STEVE FALLON was born in Boston, Massachusetts, a city on the same latitude as Rome, not Ireland as he had always assumed. He graduated from Georgetown University in 1975 with a Bachelor of Science in modern languages and then taught English in Poland. After working for several years for a newspaper in Wilmington, Delaware, and obtaining a master's degree in journalism, his interest in the 'new' Asia took him to Hong Kong, where he lived and worked for thirteen years for a variety of publications. In 1987 he put journalism on hold and opened Wanderlust Books, Asia's only travel bookshop. He lived in Budapest for two and a half years before moving to London in 1994. He has written and contributed to a number of Lonely Planet titles.

HOME
with
ALICE

A Journey in Gaelic Ireland

Steve Fallon

LONELY PLANET PUBLICATIONS
Melbourne • Oakland • London • Paris

Home with Alice: A Journey in Gaelic Ireland

Published by Lonely Planet Publications
    Head Office: 90 Maribyrnong Street, Footscray, Vic 3011, Australia
                     Locked Bag 1, Footscray, Vic 3011, Australia
    Branches: 150 Linden Street, Oakland CA 94607, USA
                     10a Spring Place, London NW5 3BH,UK
                     1 rue Dahomey, 75011, Paris, France

Published 2002
Printed by SNP SPrint (M) Sdn Bhd
Printed in Malaysia

Edited by Meaghan Amor
Maps by Natasha Velleley
Designed by Margaret Jung
Author photograph by D.J. McKinlay

National Library of Australia Cataloguing-in-Publication entry

Fallon, Steve.
  Home with Alice: a journey in Gaelic Ireland.

  Bibliography.
  ISBN 1 74059 038 4.

  Fallon, Steve, – Journeys. 2. Irish language – Social
  aspects. 3. Ireland – Description and travel. I. Title.

914.17

Text © Steve Fallon 2002
Maps © Lonely Planet 2002

LONELY PLANET and th[e]
Planet Publications Pty. Ltd

All rights reserved. No part
a retrieval system or trans
mechanical, photocopying,
the purpose of review, with

WEST SUSSEX COUNTY COUNCIL	
103226047	
Cypher	20.05.02
914.17104 B FAL	£6.99
SN9/04 RN04/05	

Alice, a chroí, tá an leabhar seo duitse.

Contents

Acknowledgements

I would like to thank my classmates in Ireland for companionship, *scéalta* and assistance, especially Kate McCormick, Sean Vanek and Anne Connon; teachers Nuala Uí Aimhirgín and Fionntán Ó Mórdha for *an Ghaeilge*; and the people of An Cheathrú Rua who continue to fight the good fight. Special thanks to Roslyn Findlay and to Neva Shaw for their helpful comments, to my sister, Maureen Fallon, who believed, and to my pole star, Michael Rothschild, who was there all along.

S.F.
London

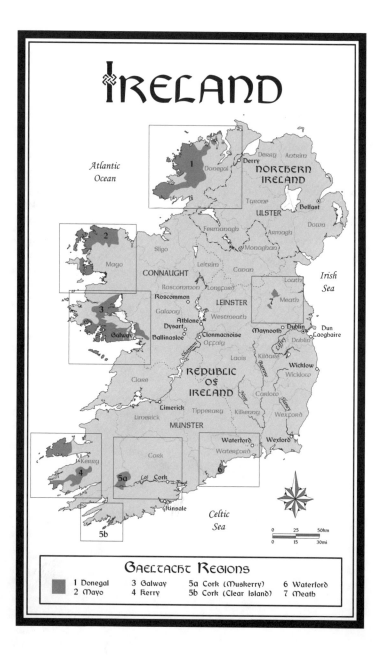

IRELAND

Atlantic
Ocean

NORTHERN
IRELAND

Derry   Antrim
Derry
Donegal

Tyrone   Belfast
ULSTER
Down

Fermanagh   Armagh
Monaghan

Sligo

Mayo   CONNAUGHT   Leitrim   Cavan

Irish
Sea

Roscommon   Longford   Louth
Roscommon
Meath

Galway   LEINSTER   Westmeath

Athlone   Maynooth   Dublin   Dun
Dysart   Caoghaire
Ballinasloe   Clonmacnoise   Dublin
Offaly

Laois   Kildare

REPUBLIC   Wicklow
OF   Wicklow
IRELAND

Clare   Carlow

Limerick   Tipperary   Kilkenny   Wexford
Limerick
MUNSTER

Waterford   Wexford
Cork   Waterford

Kerry
Lee   Cork
Cork

Kinsale   Celtic
Sea

0   25   50km
0   15   30mi

GAELTACHT REGIONS

1 Donegal	3 Galway	5a Cork (Muskerry)	6 Waterford
2 Mayo	4 Kerry	5b Cork (Clear Island)	7 Meath

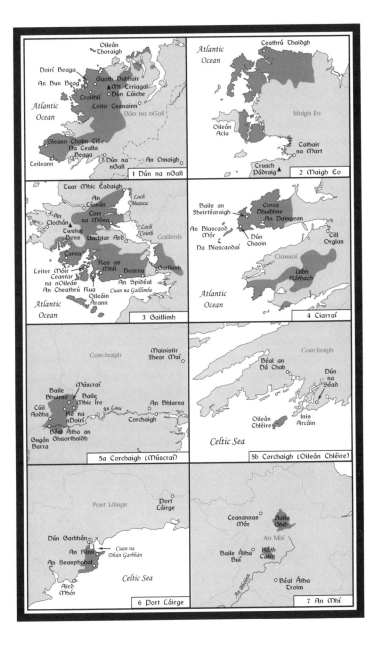

1 Dún na nGall

Oileán Thoraigh
Doirí Beaga
An Bun Beag
Gaoth Dobhair
Mt. Errigal
Dún Lúiche
Croithlí
Leitir Ceanainn
Dún na nGall
Atlantic Ocean
Gleann Cholm Cille
Na Cealla Beaga
Teileann
Dún na nGall
An Omaigh

2 Maigh Eo

Atlantic Ocean
Ceathrú Thaidhg
Maigh Eo
Oileán Acla
Cathair na Mart
Cruach Phádraig

3 Gaillimh

Tuar Mhic Éadaigh
An Clonán
Loch Measca
An Clochán
Corr na Móna
Twelve Bens
Uachtar Ard
Loch Coirib
Gaillimh
Carna
Ros an Mhíl
Bearna
Gaillimh
Leiter Móir
Ceantar na nOileán
An Cheathrú Rua
An Spidéal
Cuan na Gaillimhe
Oileáin Árann
Atlantic Ocean

4 Ciarraí

Baile an Fheirtéaraigh
Corca Dhuibhne
An Daingean
An Blascaod Mór
Dún Chaoin
Cúil Orglan
Na Blascaodaí
Ciarraí
Uíbh Ráthach
Atlantic Ocean

5a Corchaigh (Múscraí)

Corchaigh
Mainistir Fhear Maí
Múscraí
Baile Bhuirne
Baile Mhic Íre
Cúil Aodha
Ré na nDoirí
An Laoi
An Bhlarna
Corchaigh
Béal Átha an Ghugán Ghaorthaidh Barra

5b Corchaigh (Oileán Chléire)

Corchaigh
Béal an Dá Chab
Dún na Séad
Oileán Chléire
Inis Arcáin
Celtic Sea

6 Port Láirge

Port Láirge
Port Láirge
Dún Garbhán
Cuan na Dhún Garbhán
An Rinn
An Seanphobal
Aird Mhór
Celtic Sea

7 An Mhí

Ceanannas Mór
Baile Ghib
An Mhí
Baile Átha Buí
Ráth Caoin
Béal Átha Troim
An Bhóinn

Ich am of Irlaunde,
Ant of the holy londe
Of Irlande.
Gode sire, pray ich the,
For of saynte charite,
Come ant daunce wyth me
In Irlaunde.

Anonymous, circa 1300

Chapter I

The Blessing

'Enormana knocker.'

'No, no, again. Say it again. *In ainm an Athar.*'

'Enormana knocker.'

'*Agus an Mhic.*'

'August a vick.'

'*Agus an Spioraid Naomh.*'

'August a spread knave.'

'*Amen.*'

'Almond.'

The woman shifted the young boy, skinny and tall for his age, off her lap and leaned forward to put away her crocheting. She had been working on a long, irregularly shaped bandage destined, she said, for the poor lepers at the Maryknoll mission in Africa. A cloth bag full of completed dressings lay at her feet, each one rolled up like a pair of socks and secured with an elastic band. 'That's enough for now,' she said. 'We'll try it again some other time.'

The woman was my Aunt Alice. I was six years old at the time and about to enter the first grade at Saint Agatha's School. Alice was teaching me how to bless myself in what she called the Gaelic.

'Do you speak the Gaelic?' I asked her anxiously. I was spellbound by the idea that two people could sit down, make unintelligible sounds together and appear to be understanding one another. I wanted to hear more of the Gaelic.

My best friend's mother had come from France – she'd married his father when he was fighting over there in the war – and she'd taught me French words like *petit lapin* and *glace*. That was good. They were really different from 'bunny rabbit' and 'ice cream'. But once I asked another mother – she was from Berlin and lived on Denmark Ave, the same street where my best friend's house was – how to say 'The grass is green' in German. *'Der Grass ist grün,'* she'd told me. I was disappointed. It sounded almost like the way we said it. I was suspicious that she didn't know how to say 'The grass is green' the real way or had forgotten how.

'Oh, no. No-one knows the Gaelic nowadays,' said Alice. 'The Irish weren't allowed to speak it. The English made it a crime to say even one word. Can you imagine that? One time your grand-mother – she was a teacher, you know, she would have loved you – said something in the Gaelic and a Black and Tan beat her with a big leather strap. They were worse than the Nazis, the English. They took everything from the Irish. Even the Gaelic.'

I had heard many stories about the terrible English before: how they'd stood aside and laughed while Irish people starved to death during the potato famine, how they didn't let the Irish have jobs (which is why they all came to America to start a new life, as my grandparents did) and, worst of all, how they outlawed the Mass and the saints, and jailed priests and beat nuns.

We had a picture book in religion class showing the commu-nists doing the same sorts of things to the fathers and the sisters. They were drawings – like comic strips almost – and the Russians had big, mean faces with long, pointy teeth and bulging eyes. In the pictures they had put the priests behind bars and were yelling at the nuns and making them go away. Some schoolchildren were weeping in the front of one picture. I didn't think I would though. I wouldn't cry for the nuns, anyway.

Maybe the English had changed since they stole the Gaelic from the Irish. They were on television a lot, and people really liked them. My parents loved watching them doing crazy things and singing funny songs on Channel 2. My mother said the English sounded ritzy when they talked. We weren't allowed to watch that program because it was on too late, she told us, but my brothers and I could hear them laughing loudly in the parlour as we lay in our beds up in the attic.

It began to rain as it often did in Boston after a hot August afternoon, and it made me feel a little sad. Alice moved to close the screen window in the porch that looked out onto Sedalia Road in Dorchester and over to the house on Elmer Road where my family lived before we moved to Milton. I wished we still lived in that house across the street from Alice so I could see her all the time. A man and a woman with a new baby lived there now.

Alice reached into her pocketbook and pulled out a pencil case. 'This is for your first day at school,' she said, handing it to me. It had little compartments for pencils and an eraser, and a snap to keep it closed. On the cover was a picture of Dorothy from *The Wizard of Oz*. Next to her was the Scarecrow, the Tin Man and the Cowardly Lion.

I liked the way Alice smiled and the way she pursed her lips when she said words like 'girl' and 'person'. I liked how she did a funny dance when she sang 'Buffalo Girls' and the way she smelled – of a perfume called 'Blue Waltz' that she kept in a large bottle with one of those rubber balls you squeezed on the top, of the Chesterfield cigarettes she smoked and of a drink of ginger ale with something sour in it that she let me taste sometimes. I liked everything about Aunt Alice.

'I love a rainy day, don't you?' she asked me. 'It makes everything feel so *teolaí*.'

That was another word she'd taught me in the Gaelic. 'Choley' didn't sound at all like 'comfy' or 'cosy'. That was good too. I liked the Gaelic and wished the English hadn't taken it away from the Irish. Maybe if I said three Hail Marys the English would give it back to the Irish and then we could speak it too. And maybe if I blessed myself with holy water - the really special holy water from Lourdes that my mother's friend had given her - they would do it really quickly.

Chapter II

In the Beginning

'I was born from love/And my poor mother worked the mines . . .'
Okay, so I've told a lie already. It isn't the first one and it won't
be the last. But when I grew older – reading, daydreaming and
beginning to wonder whether grown-ups like Alice knew as much
as I had thought they did – I'd pretend that the opening lyrics
from that old Laura Nyro song 'Stony End' described my arrival
here on God's green earth. A little scandal, a few dark secrets,
something disreputable – anything but nine pounds, nine ounces,
of pink flesh wrapped in a blue blanket and driven home to sub-
urbia in a four-door Chevrolet. I wanted to be something different, even if it just meant making the words to the song my own
while listening to the stereo.

Now whether or not me or any of my four siblings were born
'from love' in the literal sense or the then ultra-scandalous figu-
rative one is really neither here nor there. This was Boston of the
mudflat 1950s and my parents, both of them the spawn of a pair
of immigrants from Ireland, were devout Catholics; to be Irish
was to be Catholic and that was that. We knew that Andrew
Jackson, Sam Houston and even Davy Crockett had all had Irish
families. But they were Scotch Irish – Protestants – and had
became not honorary but fully fledged WASPs as soon as they hit
the shores of America.

Catholic marriage was all about children – as many or as few
as God ordained. There was little discussion, decision-making or
planning. And at the risk of committing a mortal sin and facing
eternal damnation, there was certainly no artificial prevention. It
either happened or it didn't.

My parents got to work almost immediately, and I know that to be a fact from a letter at the bottom of a box of memories stored somewhere up in the attic of the old house in Milton. Shortly after they had been married at Saint Brendan's Church on Gallivan Boulevard in Dorchester, my mother and father both contracted the flu. A particularly virulent strain it was too for they were both sent to the hospital.

My father must have been beside himself with worry, both for his new bride and himself, in between bouts of delirium-inducing fever and all the aches and pains. Thirty years before, his father had died at almost the same age when a great influenza epidemic had swept across much of the world. My grandfather had left behind a pregnant wife and four sons, all under the age of six.

After my father had been discharged and sent home, he wrote an encouraging and very loving get-well note to my mother, who remained in her sick bed at the Carney Hospital on Dorchester Ave. He told her about meeting her sister Alice by chance a couple of days before as she walked down the hill from the subway station at Ashmont to Sedalia Road. 'Rita had better hurry up and get better,' he quoted her as having told him. 'There's still plenty of unfinished business to attend to.' My father had underlined Alice's words and added a few exclamation points. Clearly there was a job at hand that required immediate attention, and they got to it. My older brother was born less than a year later.

'The mine' in the song would have taxed the imagination of even the greatest of pretenders and I was just a novice at the time. Even if my mother had been forced (for economic reasons or so that I could claim those lyrics as my own) to take up a pickaxe like a Molly Maguire, she would have had to travel pretty far. Not counting the Quincy quarries, where we used to jump naked from the huge granite blocks into pools of rainwater on hot summer days, the closest mine must have been a thousand miles away from where we lived.

No, Mrs Thomas Fallon was 'just a housewife' as most mothers in our neighbourhood described themselves in those days, without a hint of embarrassment or the need for any justification.

'Housewife' was the word used only in conversation, though. It became 'homemaker' when they filled out official forms or applications. Mothers who worked full-time were teachers or nurses, jobs that commanded respect. The few who had attended college, even for just a short time, had the highest status of all. Education ranked just below Catholicism but higher than the Democratic Party in the league tables of homage and respect. A woman who lived on Berlin Ave had a Master's degree. She was considered just short of divine.

My father was a bus driver, which became 'bus operator' on those same forms and applications that homemakers filled in. It was a job that carried no particular status, but it was like the work of the fathers of all the other kids. No doctors, lawyers or Indian chiefs lived in our neighbourhood; it was where policemen, truck drivers and the odd insurance salesman raised their families.

No-one was rich and no-one was poor in the area where we lived. All the men worked unless they were retired or invalids. We all received Christmas presents and birthday gifts, spent a couple of weeks of each summer in crowded little rented cottages on the beaches of Cape Cod or in the mountains of New Hampshire, and got weekly allowances for the household chores we did. That would have all been accomplished on one salary that almost never rose above four digits. We all referred to ourselves as middle class.

Most of the families around us were large and had Irish names, immigrants in the great wave that washed so many urban dwellers from the cities of north-east America into the suburbs after World War II. That you were Irish and Catholic were the two things generally taken for granted here, and we knew all about everyone who wasn't one or the other: the German woman on Denmark Ave, my best friend (well, he was *half* Irish and, of course, Catholic), the Protestant family at the end of Hope Ave who never went to church. None of these things was ever discussed. They were just known.

Even if we happened to find ourselves in a house in an unfamiliar part of town (as unlikely as that sounds, trick-or-treating at Halloween had avaricious kids roaming pretty far and wide on their own in those days), we'd expect to see a portrait of President Kennedy with the First Lady, Jackie, Pope John XXIII and/or the Sacred Heart hanging in a prominent place somewhere on the wall.

One late afternoon during the build-up to Christmas, we saw the mother of a kid who had just moved onto Collamore Street lighting a large candelabrum on the kitchen table. We thought the new family was rich; all the candles made the room look like a scene from one of those movies our parents watched on 'The Late Show', with men wearing tuxedos and women in long gowns sitting around a large piano drinking cocktails. The new kid, Joey, told us that it was called a menorah and that they lit the candles to celebrate Chanukah. We were excited to learn how different he was and bombarded him with questions. Did the Jews really kill Jesus? Did he only believe in God the Father? What about the Holy Ghost? (We didn't understand much about the white bird with the halo ourselves but thought it had a wicked cool name.) Was he going to have a tree and get presents on Chanukah Day?

We didn't feel any animosity or chauvinism toward those who didn't fit into the Irish and Catholic categories, only curiosity. Why would we? We were in the majority here in suburban Boston; it would be years before I'd even hear the terms 'Mick' and 'Paddy' used and it would be far from home. In any case, everyone around us was at least a New Englander and an American (usually thought of in that order). Being something different from any of those things was pretty neat.

Many Americans, even those living overseas, still feel the need to place one another in categories when they meet for the first time. Not so much by class but by ethnic origin. Britons and Australians, among others, are forever surprised when they hear two Americans new to one another asking each other's nationality. 'But you're both Yanks,' they say. 'Can't you hear it?' Of course we can. We know we're Americans, but we're also Poles or Italians or 'a little bit French, a quarter Lebanese, some Scotch Irish and one-eighth Cherokee'. In a composite culture like America's, that has always seemed to make a difference.

I can remember wanting to be different from a very young age. Not not Catholic. I would never have wished not to be a member of the only true religion, as we were told it was. To do that was to blaspheme against the one holy and apostolic Church, and I would have been damned to the punishment of hell for all eternity, unless I confessed my mortal sin to the priest in the little booth in church on Saturday afternoon, something I could never, ever, do. I would have been too scared of Father Reilly's reaction. He gave us the usual penance – three Our Fathers, three Hail Marys, a string of ejaculations – for things like being unkind to our younger sisters or disobeying our parents, but he got very angry and made us say whole rosaries if we confessed to impure thoughts or taking nickels and dimes from our mothers' purses. Sometimes he even shouted, which everyone waiting in the pews outside could hear. I couldn't bear to think how he'd react if I told him I no longer wanted to go to confession, receive the Holy Eucharist or mumble Latin prayers I didn't understand while kneeling beside him on the altar at the start of Mass.

It was ordinary and boring to be Irish like everybody else though, and praying to be a different nationality and to acquire the physical features that went along with it wasn't even a venial sin, at least as far as I knew. I didn't like having straight blond hair or pale skin that changed to the angry hue of a boiled Maine lobster when I sat for too long on Wollaston Beach or didn't wear a hat while caddying at the local golf course. I wanted the black curls that the Roman soldiers in our ancient history textbook had spilling out of whiskbroom helmets onto their foreheads. I imagined myself with a nose shaped like my parakeet's beak and a complexion that they called 'olive' for some reason or another. It didn't look anything like the little green pellets stuffed with red bits that my father brought home in a slender jar before company arrived. That colour of skin looked like gold to me.

From the library I borrowed a Landmark book about an archaeologist, something I wanted to be when I grew up but only if it included learning foreign languages too. The archaeologist wrote that when he was a boy and had finished reading his first book about ancient Greece, 'I wept the entire night because I was not Greek'. I wasn't going to cry about being Irish – tears didn't come easily to me anyway – but I knew what he meant. We were Catholics. We had prayer when we wanted something.

We lived in East Milton, the part of town bordering Dorchester and all the triple-decker wooden houses where the parents of many of us had been born. From our vantage point, everything else in town was 'the other side of Milton', the right side of the tracks, where Boston Brahmin types lived in old mansions with huge lawns on a hill overlooking the Neponset River, and Jewish doctors and lawyers raised their families in modern split-level houses that sometimes even had swimming pools. It would be a while before that great leveller, public high school, would bring all these disparate groups together, before the kids from East Milton Square – an intersection of several streets with a five-and-ten-cent store, a grocery, a bowling alley, a drug store with a soda fountain and a fire station – saw how the other half spent their time and allowances in the quainter, more affluent Milton Village in Lower Mills. They had antique stores and even a coffee shop.

Until we began boarding the crowded yellow bus bound for Milton High School, almost every schoolchild in our area attended Saint Agatha's, the Catholic elementary school next to the parish church and fronted by a large parking lot to accommodate the enormous finned and winged vehicles of the faithful. Taking pride of place on the east side of the lot was a group of almost life-sized statues that looked like they were made from shiny white marble but felt rough, almost like sandpaper, when you touched them on a dare. They were of the Virgin Mary and the three young Portuguese shepherds to whom she had appeared at Fatima in 1917; the leg of one of the lambs at their feet had been broken off and I wondered how long the kid who had done it would spend in purgatory.

No-one seemed to know why that particular incarnation of the Virgin had been chosen for a predominantly Irish Catholic parish, but it was a good one for kids to play guessing games with. Mary had told the children three secrets. Playground lore had it that the pope fainted when he sneaked a peek into the envelope or wherever the secrets were kept. It had to be something really scary.

The Fatima statues were the focal point of the May Procession, Saint Agatha's largest and most important annual event, in which Our Lady was enthroned as Queen of the Rosary with a floral crown. It was a formal and solemn occasion – a pageant really – and everyone attending the school was expected to dress in the outfit of their affiliation: cassock and surplice for altar boys, uniforms for scouts, white dress or suit for the second-graders making their first Holy Communion, red robes for those who'd been confirmed that spring. Everyone else sported satin capes slung jauntily over their shoulders. Though coveted, the violet, blue and green capes indicated that the wearers did not belong to any particular group; they were just 'the others'. It seemed to me that very few people at Saint Agatha's wanted not to belong and even if the colourful garments proved too much of a temptation, there would be no possibility of denying affiliations. The nuns, with their 360 degree vision, knew all.

Our teachers were members of the Congregation of Saint Joseph, or CSJ as it appeared below the signature of the nun who signed our report cards or disciplinary notes sent home to our parents requiring their presence – along with ours – at evening conferences held at the convent. That happened to me once. I'd been misbehaving again, talking out of turn, passing notes to friends, not giving my best effort to my studies and, worst, I'd answered Sister Antoinette back when she'd called me to task for my crimes.

I sweated out the day, my stomach churning every time I thought of my mother's reaction to the note I'd been told to give her. I knew my father wouldn't make too much of a fuss about it, but I was certain my mother would be furious. As was common in the Irish Catholic households in our neighbourhood, my mother was the disciplinarian; there were no threats of 'wait until your father comes home' in our house. My mother would have taken care of that well before my father returned.

Again and again I thought about ripping up the note and running away. The problem with my plan was that I didn't have the bus fare, and my mother held the bankbook to the savings account where I'd deposited the money I'd earned caddying. In the end I decided that my only real option was to deliver the note, and I was relieved by my mother's reaction. Both my parents were sympathetic but stern on the way up Father Carney Drive to the massive house where the two dozen nuns lived together, but once we'd crossed the threshold and faced my accuser and judge, they acted more like us than them. 'Yes, Sister,' they said, nodding their heads, then 'No, Sister', and shaking them as Sister Antoinette spouted a litany of things I should be doing and an even longer one of what I should not be doing, while I was ordered to stand at attention.

The nuns had 'given up their lives for God', my mother told me as we drove home. They were 'the brides of Christ' and deserved our respect and total obedience at all times. During the day they were our surrogate parents and our guardians in matters of faith and morals. They were not to be questioned, much less defied.

It was an education very much part of the old school, where we learned to 'respect' (read fear) authority, and some of the nuns embraced this power as though it were Jesus incarnate Himself, forever locked in a dance of discipline, humiliation and favouritism. I danced with enough of these twisted sisters at Saint Agatha's to conclude early on that even if they had been marginalised by society at a time when horizons were pretty low for most middle-class women, they would be monsters in or out of their habits.

Of course, not all the nuns left their charges scorched, torn or less than whole. Many were fully suited to their vocations as teachers in a religious community and were inspirational, encouraging, charitable and fair. These are the nuns that many of us who endured Catholic elementary education would like to remember. Sadly, they compete in our memories with the termagants and vixens impossible to forget.

Catholic school life was inextricably bound to the cycle of the liturgical year: from Advent and its wreaths and calendars, with tantalising little doors covering each date, to Christmas; through the fasting, giving up favourite foods or pastimes, and the appearance of church statues cocooned in the purple cloths of Lent, to Easter.

We attended Mass every Sunday and on all Holy Days of Obligation, of course; some really religious families went to church every day during Lent. We all received the sacraments – communion and penance in second grade, confirmation in sixth – that were explained in question and answer format in the *Baltimore Catechism*, the book of all knowledge that we'd parrot in religion class. There were novenas to Saint Francis Xavier in March and special blessings, too, such as the one on the feast day of Saint Blaise in early February when the priest would hold crossed candles in front of the throats of the faithful to ward off colds, flu and errant fish bones.

Confirmation, in which we were inducted as 'soldiers of Christ', was probably the sacrament we got most excited about. Not only was there the much-feared slap on the cheek from the bishop, reminding us that as Catholics we had to suffer for our faith, we also got to choose another name to place behind our first and middle ones.

We had to pick a saint's name – Wendy or Wayne was not

acceptable – and the choice was enormous. There was at least one for every day of the year and sometimes more: doctors of the church such as Thomas Aquinas, Jerome, Francis de Sales and Augustine, mystics like Teresa of Avila and John of the Cross, apostles, abbots, confessors, deacons and virgins. And then there was the panoply of martyrs, Christians who had endured unspeakable blood-fests at the hands of the Romans and others, and died, almost never in one piece, for the glory of God. The breasts of Agatha, the patron of our school, were lopped off; Lucy had her eyes plucked out. Laurence was fried on a gridiron and such was his faith that he cheerfully asked to be turned over after one side had been sufficiently roasted. Sebastian met his end punctured like a pincushion by arrows, while the unnamed First Martyrs of the Church of Rome were tied up in animal skins and set before starving dogs.

These gory stories were as familiar to us as the promise of heaven, the threat of hell and the likelihood of purgatory. Though they were meant to inspire us, to remind us that we too could achieve sainthood if we suffered for our faith, I don't think most of us believed for a moment that we'd endure more than a pinch if the Russians invaded Milton and put us to the test. Instead we read and listened to these tales of blood and guts with both fear and fascination. Other saints, like Elizabeth of Hungary, had lived exemplary lives of prayer, fasting and the requisite bit of self-flagellation, but they sounded ordinary in comparison to those toasted and diced for their God. The Irish saints like Patrick, Bridget, Columba and Brendan sailed and preached and did funny things with shamrocks and snakes, but there wasn't a martyr among them. They were nice and they were boring.

The congregation at Saint Agatha's was not entirely Irish – there was a sprinkling of Italians and the Heinz types of mixed nationality – but it often felt that way. The Catholic Church at large felt Irish in the days when the cardinal was called Cushing and Mass

13

on Saint Patrick's Day was as well attended as those on holy days like the Assumption and All Saints' Day. On the feast of the Glorious Apostle of Ireland, everyone wore green and was an honorary Irish citizen for the day.

Saint Patrick's Day was not an official holiday in our town, but it was in Boston. It wasn't actually meant to honour Saint Patrick as such. There it was called Evacuation Day and marked the anniversary of the day the British left Boston in 1776 after being defeated by George Washington. Bostonians were proud that they'd whipped the redcoats so early on in the Revolution, but they all knew the real reason why they had 17 March off work and school. A great Saint Patrick's Day parade was held in Southie – South Boston – that we were all anxious to attend but never could.

Apart from Saint Patrick's Day, weddings, which came as regularly as the snow fell in winter, were the times when many Irish wore their nationality most prominently in public. All the familiar traits – the legacies from the Old Country – were on full display: conviviality and verbosity, to be sure, along with a certain morbidity, depression and alcoholism. Songs, drinks, jocular tales and boisterous laughter could dissolve into arguments, tears and sometimes physical fights; it was like a play being acted out on stage or a year's worth of events squeezed into a single afternoon.

Wakes were as common as weddings, and my father seemed to go to one a week, offering condolences to the friends and family of people he barely knew. They were generally sombre occasions, but an Irish wake is an Irish wake and the goings-on when highballs were served in the kitchen might not be unlike those at an Irish wedding.

Beyond this patina of song and booze; parades where the colour green dominated; church-sponsored trips to Knock and the Ring of Kerry; and the annual Irish Sweepstakes, when the priest in the pulpit would suspend the venial sin of gambling because it was for a good cause (the hospitals of Ireland), there wasn't really very much else that we could claim was specifically Irish about us. Most of the Italians we knew had their own food, their language in a jumbled, broken sort of way and relatives 'back home' with whom they kept in sporadic contact and even visited over the course of the years. No-one Irish in our neighbourhood had any-thing of the first two, and very few had the last. It was as if our grandparents had stripped off their Irish clothes as soon as they'd stepped off the boat at the docks in East Boston and donned new ones, ridding themselves in the process of the lice of poverty, the memories of one-horse towns going nowhere and everything and everyone in them.

Detached from the Old Country, recent arrivals also took on this hybrid Irish-American identity, quickly losing themselves in a jumble of memories. Smoky pubs with earthen floors, session music and set dancing were exchanged for corner bars with neon lights, 'When Irish Eyes Are Smiling' and the twist, the rocks of Connemara forgotten for the Blarney Stone. Saint Patrick's Day, traditionally a quiet holiday in Ireland when people sported a green ribbon or a spray of shamrocks in their lapels, became even for these newcomers a day of national focus and pride, with 'Kiss Me, I'm Irish' buttons pinned to baseball caps and green beer gushing from barroom taps.

The best of the Old Country was dusted off from time to time for glorification and then put away for another viewing at some later date. Once my father took me to a slide show of Ireland's riches – megalithic tombs, the River Shannon and all the lakes, the Book of Kells – hosted by a popular radio DJ at a Catholic girls' school near us. It went on for hours and we were all nod-ding off as the DJ droned on. One slide was of a large brooch that had been worked on both sides. This was an example of the Irish 'striving for perfection', the DJ said. I wondered why someone would bother decorating the side of a pin that no-one could see. I thought it was stupid.

The only thing Irish I remember about my father's mother, the one grandparent I'd arrived in time to meet, is that she baked soda bread on rare occasions in a massive cast-iron stove that looked like it might have still burned turf. The bread was dry, with a rock-hard heel and tasted of salt – not a patch on the cotton-white Wonder Bread my mother bought to make the tuna fish and baloney sandwiches we'd carry to school in our lunchboxes. My grandmother spoke in a soft voice with a pronounced Boston accent, not even a hint of a brogue, and she never mentioned Ireland or anything Irish for that matter. It wasn't surprising; little Molly had been a child when her parents, Patrick and Hanorah Costello, had brought her to America. In her case it would have been more a question of not knowing much – if anything at all – about the Old Country than wanting or trying to forget.

She did once tell us something about her husband, Bernard, our grandfather who had died so young, leaving her to raise a large family on her own. He'd been born in the same hardscrabble town in County Roscommon as she had, and shortly after they were engaged, he returned to Ireland to ensure he was making the right decision about marrying and raising a family in a new land. She mustn't have had any doubt that he'd return because she asked him to buy her a china dinner service. He brought back a set of sombre brown and white dishes, plates, cups and saucers that took pride of place in a glass cabinet in her dining room. They were the last fragile link to the land of their birth, a memorial to something gone and a past no longer remembered. I can't recall them ever being used.

Aunt Alice, herself born and raised in America well after her parents had arrived from County Cork, was the one who carried the Irish banner in our family, unfurling and waving it when she felt the occasion demanded. She was the strongest link to an Ireland remembered through the haze of years, and she saw it as her task to keep our Irish identity – such as it was – alive. Alice was hardly *Hibernis ipsis Hiberniores* – 'more Irish than the Irish themselves' – as many of the early invaders had themselves become after settling in Ireland. She knew little about the country, beyond what her mother had told her and how the memories had been transformed into Irish-American culture. In her lifetime, she never had the chance to visit Ireland.

Alice alone could remember all the words to songs like 'Galway Bay' and 'Little Town in the Old County Down'. She'd sing them after a few drinks at weddings and parties in a high-pitched, reedy voice, usually in a duet with one of my uncles, who would mouth the few lyrics they knew and then hum along for the rest. She told us stories – she was the quintessential storyteller – about the 'lace curtain Irish' of Boston, and immigrants like the Kennedys and Fitzgeralds who had managed to get 'inside' and up the stairs to affluence and fame (or notoriety), despite the signs reading 'No Irish Need Apply' or 'No Irish, No Catholics' on the door. She could do an 'Oirish' accent that would be at home in a Connacht country town and could pull up all kinds of mysterious expressions from the well of words left behind by her parents and grandparents. 'County Mayo, God save us!' she'd say when someone 'full of malarkey' was telling her tales that she thought had been too highly seasoned or was 'crying poor mouth' again. 'Don't tread on the tail of me coat', she'd say when someone was bothering her.

Neither Alice nor anyone else we knew had the Gaelic though. Apart from the sign of the cross and the odd mispronounced word that had lodged in some tight space in our family's collective memory – 'awmadawn' (*amadán*) for a fool or a dullard, or 'kaw-togue' (*ciothóg*) for someone left-handed – the language was no more a part of us than the swimming pools and mansions on the other side of Milton. The only time we ever saw anything of the Gaelic was on Saint Patrick's Day, when people wore buttons with the words '*Erin go bragh*', or 'Ireland Forever', which I would later discover was a kind of hybrid Irish-American phrase never used in Ireland, or on a greeting card with '*beannachtaí*', or 'bless-ings', bestowed upon the recipient. Many people, including Alice, thought the language had died out altogether and existed only in a few old songs and a limited choice of Hallmark greeting cards.

I'd been keen on language from an early age, starting with my own. Once, after one of the first few days at kindergarten, I asked my mother what a minnow was. When she told me, I couldn't for the life of me figure out why we were singing about 'a little fish' while reciting the alphabet: 'Ella minnow pee . . .' And if my mother read *Rita's Digest* each month, did other mothers have magazines named after them too?

Foreign languages intrigued me. I didn't concentrate on any one in a disciplined fashion and learn it step by step, but dipped in and out of anything I could borrow from the Milton Public Library. I'd memorised the Cyrillic alphabet from a Russian grammar hidden beneath my science book in fifth grade and had come to terms with at least the concept of three genders in German. It wasn't long before I learned that the Irish language had not in fact followed the same route taken by Latin and the dodo bird. It lived on in the Gaeltacht, the collective name for the small districts in remote parts of Ireland where people still washed the dishes, played cards and made their plans in the Gaelic.

My father worked with a man much younger than himself who had come to Boston from Dingle in the Kerry Gaeltacht. Mike, who was about to return to Ireland to take charge of the family farm, hadn't been raised speaking the language, but he'd grown up among people who had and he understood some of it. He taught me a few words, but they were hard to pronounce and didn't sound anything like the way they were written down. 'It's a dying language,' he told me. 'Soon only the old people will know it, and when they go it will disappear altogether.'

Once, in my early teens, I was foraging through the swollen stacks of the Boston Public Library in Copley Square when I came across a book whose title interested me as much as its contents: *Irish Without Tears*. It was a Gaelic grammar written for students in Ireland who were required to study the language in school but, judging from its title, were apparently not enjoying the task. In junior high school a lot of my fellow students disliked studying French and Spanish, finding it difficult to get their heads around verb tenses that we didn't have in English and the idea that nouns could be masculine or feminine. They argued that they'd never have any need for it anyway. I disagreed, putting mathematics in that category. But I wondered: was Irish so difficult and such a drudge as to induce tears?

I didn't cry over it – the book had promised me I wouldn't after all – but I was frightened by all the vowels clustered together, even in the language's name, *Gaeilge*, and the unsightly groups of consonants like 'bhf' and 'gc' that were supposed to sound like 'w' and 'k'. That the simple phrase 'in Boston' could turn out looking like '*i mBoston*' and be pronounced 'ee moston' baffled me. How could anyone read – much less speak – a language so complicated, so ancient-looking and impenetrable? I didn't even get halfway through the first lesson when I closed the book and returned it to the library.

While many other languages, ones with which I had no special bond or sometimes even practical use for, would later germinate and flower whenever I watered and nurtured them, Irish stayed locked away in the dark room where I'd left it, and I wouldn't open that door again for many years. I may have been lazy or uninterested; perhaps I was surprised that I wasn't even able to pronounce a few words that my ancestors would have been babbling with ease by the time they were off the floor and standing upright. I had no regrets leaving it behind though. It had never been mine in the first place.

There are people who say that part of the resistance to learning or speaking Irish in the past has been based in guilt. The descendants of those who lost the ability to speak their own language, who abandoned it under pressure or by choice, feel a sense of shame, they say, not dissimilar to the remorse of neglecting or deserting a child. They wish to shut out the memory within themselves and sometimes in others too.

There might be some truth to that, but the fact that the language was difficult and was presented in such an archaic fashion in the book I'd borrowed certainly discouraged me. At the same time, though, I was rebelling against Irish-American culture and all its associations, including Catholicism. The rituals and the ceremonies, the dressing up and reciting prayers in Latin had been comforting, even entertaining, when I was young, something with which to identify myself.

Martyrs and stigmatics don't make good travelling companions for young adults, and as I grew older and people around me began to get further involved with the Church, I'd already moved far away from it all. I didn't care about a new Mass said in English by a pinched-face Italian pope, the Knights of Columbus, hand-knitted Aran sweaters ordered by mail, taverns with cute names like the Eire Pub or the Shamrock Inn or the precise difference between the Immaculate Conception and the Virgin Birth. If anything, I found it all embarrassing and would joke about it, arguing only half in jest that Ireland owed us all compensation for dominating the Catholic Church in America and putting us all through such torture over the years. By the time I left home for university, being Irish or Catholic weren't ways I defined myself any longer. In fact, they didn't feel very much like parts of me at all.

Chapter III

Epiphany

'Everyone returns to kind in the end,' a close friend is fond of saying. She finds it reassuring to believe that her circles within circles of friends – most of whom have wandered pretty far from where they began their journeys long before – won't still be roaming when it's time to check in their bags permanently.

Whether or not that's true is debatable; I'm not sure I'd find it comforting even if it were. People might go back to where it all began for them, but I don't suppose many of them stay for very long. Most have the habit of trying on new clothes as they go along and it suits them; different outfits can feel as comfortable and look as smart as the old ones once did. They keep them on and reinvent themselves. They become new people – or at least they think they have.

Everyone I met at university was studying languages or something to do with international relations. Such disciplines belonged to a very wide world and the possibilities for reinvention were limitless. It's not surprising that many of my fellow students wanted to change more than just their shirts upon arrival.

During my first week at Georgetown I became friendly with an English 'lad', as he called himself. Well, he said he was from England. From Plymouth, in fact. 'You know, old chap, the place where your Pilgrims left from.' That impressed me. I'd thought most Britons, most Europeans, couldn't be bothered with American history. I assumed they thought it was all too recent and not much more than a string of presidential terms, expanding borders and armed interventions. He had the haircut, he had the clothes and he had the accent at a time when it was the height of cool to look and sound like you were from the other side of the Atlantic. And when we asked him about all those wars – the American Revolution and World War II being the most popular ones – and about rock groups and the royal family, he knew all the answers.

He told us that his mother was American and his father a British diplomat and that they'd decided to send him to America for his secondary education so that he could enter the School of Foreign Service at Georgetown. When he revealed he'd attended Boston College High School my status was instantly raised among the other students in the dormitory – we were now related by civic pride. He and I got to share impressions of my home-town and the city where he'd spent the previous four years. 'The Hub of the Universe', 'the Athens of America', more universities and colleges than any other place in the country . . . We both knew all the superlatives and boasts and why progressive and ultra-cultured Bean Town was superior to Washington and maybe even New York.

When I went back to Boston for the Christmas vacation I couldn't wait to tell my friend, Michael, who had graduated from B.C. High the previous spring, about having met his English former classmate. I wanted to ask him whether they too had compared American and British culture, discussed history and become friends.

Michael was surprised when I mentioned my new mate's name. 'Luke Dayton? The Luke Dayton who graduated with me in June?' he asked. 'English? You nerd, Luke Dayton's not English! He's from Salem or some place like that.' My new English buddy was just another kid from the North Shore trying to reinvent himself and not covering all the bases in the process.

I stopped being Irish after I left home. Not entirely, but it certainly wasn't at the top of the list of ways I defined myself. How Irish was I anyway? I had the propensity to drink more than I

should, to dream and to tell stories – in both senses of the word
– but not much else. I never denied my heritage – why would I?
– but there were just too many other interesting choices and new
prospects available when I finally stepped out into the world.
Everything seems possible when you're young, including
becoming someone or something new. I might not have tried to
pretend to be a completely different person like Luke Dayton,
but as I began to move around a bit more I sometimes came
closer than I thought I ever would.

Languages can lead people to new identities; it gives them a
sense of belonging. Sometimes languages perform these tricks
without the learners even realising it. Those new to a language
might pick up a gesture – a flick of the finger, a nod of the head –
or different facial expressions as they traipse through unfamiliar
intonation or express shock, glee or indignation in their borrowed
tongue. It's not uncommon to see *gaijins* (foreigners) in Tokyo
bowing as they talk to a superior in Japanese, even while on the
telephone. For all intents and purposes, they have become
Japanese. Foreigners living in Italy may wave their hand back over
their shoulders to signify the past. A Gallic shrug can be had only
by reaching the degree of arrogance that is unique to France. It's
not the easiest of foreign gestures to acquire; it comes only when
foreigners have become as French as *les français* themselves.

I spent a year studying in France once, and I too became
French for a time. Whenever I had a chance to leave the country,
which was often since class attendance was not mandatory and
lecture notes were freely available, I became even more French.
When I'd ditch all my lectures and hitchhike to places like
Munich or Prague in winter, I'd be from Paris. The truck drivers
who ferried me across Germany never spoke French and assumed
'the Frenchman' didn't speak any German beyond '*Wo gehen Sie,
bitte?*' Instead they'd try out their English on me. We'd talk at
length high up in the warm cab, sharing snacks and sandwiches
and shouting over the roar of the autobahn traffic. They'd always
compliment me on my English. I enjoyed being something new
and different and tried to figure out how to stay that way.

After I left university I taught English in Silesia in south-west Poland, a place where it was just as easy and rewarding being who I really was than someone else. In a dirty but relatively affluent coal-mining town like Katowice, anyone from the West was new and different, sought out and overindulged; it was not exactly a city under siege by tourists. This was especially true for Americans. Virtually everyone I'd meet seemed to have relatives in Chicago and wanted to know whether I'd met them along the way.

I didn't want or need to be a Chicagoan. I was too busy discovering who I really was and what I'd come to like. Adding new forms of identity to my real self was a lot more fun than making them up.

Not long after I returned to America to settle into a 'real' job, I met someone who would subsequently share all my identities and help me discover and take on new ones along the way. It was a winter afternoon and piles of dirty snow were banked up along the curb. I was sliding along the icy sidewalks of Spruce Street, dragging a large cardboard box full of laundry that I'd just finished washing and thinking about Gary Gilmore standing in front of a firing squad that morning. A pair of bright eyes met mine from below a woollen cap.

Mike liked that I had lived in Poland and was fair; he guessed that I was Irish. I liked that he was Jewish, had the dark curls I coveted and planned to study Chinese at university. And we wanted each other. By the time we'd reached the warmth of my tiny studio, it was clear that we were both looking to satisfy more than just hunger, and we talked and talked about the past and then the future, until just before his last train to the suburbs was about to depart.

The last train began to leave regularly without Mike, and after a while we were free to make plans about where we wanted to go and how we were going to get there. We went to Hong Kong and stayed for a much longer time than we'd intended, working as writers and journalists and acquiring a taste for Asia so deep and fundamental that our bones will be dust before it dies. Hong Kong was our life, rice was our staple and I still avoid the number four considered so unlucky by the Chinese. But those were years of great change, and we grew tired of sitting in the same chair. We moved on and found our way to Budapest, a city and culture in rapid transformation and one that seemed to suit our temperaments.

The world I lived in then was a great distance from where I'd started. It was easy to check in with the past though by going back to Boston to visit family and friends from time to time. Irish America didn't feel like home, but it wasn't boring, awkward or foreign by any means. I'd made all my own choices already and we'd be making a lot more decisions together in the future. Irish America was in the past and wouldn't play a role in any of them.

Once, on holiday in Ireland, I stepped further back in time, something I'd never considered doing before. It all happened by accident, and I was surprised at both what I found and how interested I was in finding it.

Mike and I had been travelling west across Ireland and had stopped at Clonmacnoise, an ancient monastic complex built on a glacial ridge overlooking the River Shannon. The abbey had been founded by Ciarán, the son of a Roscommon chariot maker and another one of those unmartyred Irish saints, in the mid-sixth century. Within 100 years it had become the most important centre of Christianity, literature and art in Ireland, and monks from all over Europe came to study and pray there. Clonmacnoise was one of the reasons Ireland became known as the 'island of saints and scholars' while much of Europe languished in the Dark Ages. Such was the monastery's importance that the high kings of Connacht and Tara were brought there for burial.

It was a beautiful spot – or so we imagined it would be if the weather hadn't been so miserable. Before we set out that morning, the woman at the B&B in Dublin had said we could expect a 'soft day'. In our language it was pouring.

We were in the visitors' centre, sheltering from the cold rain and wind of a July afternoon, when I came across a large atlas of Ireland in the bookshop. 'Hey, look at this,' I called out to Mike, who was browsing wistfully through a selection of walking guides and turning to watch the rain lash the ancient church stones and high crosses outside. 'I want to show you the town where my grandparents were born.' Mike was interested in genealogy and family backgrounds but had to enjoy them vicariously. Records of his family, who originated in eastern Germany and Lithuania, were scant or non-existent. The ever-changing borders of Central and Eastern Europe, World War II and the Holocaust had seen to that. His family's collective memory of where they'd come from could probably have been put into a couple of sentences.

I knew the name of the town where my paternal grandparents had been born – my grandmother had told me it when I was a child – but I'd never actually located it on a map. I suppose I was interested in knowing where and how my ancestors lived, but our links to Ireland had been severed so many years before that there didn't seem to be much point in investigating it. There were no communal memories of the place, no relatives that we knew about and Roscommon – landlocked, flat and lacking in the ancient sites scattered throughout most of the rest of Ireland – just didn't seem to have the cachet that places like Galway, Kerry and Donegal did. I'd never met anyone who had anything – much less anything nice – to say about County Roscommon.

In the atlas there was no entry in County Roscommon for the town whose name I'd remembered from so long ago. It appeared in some other areas of Ireland, and I tried every spelling variation I could think of. Mike suggested I may have got the name wrong or remembered it incorrectly.

'The name of the town of Dysart in Roscommon was the sole Irish legacy left to me by the only Irish-born grandparent I ever knew,' I told him with mock indignation. 'That's impossible.' I don't think he was convinced.

'You won't be finding the name Dysart on a map,' a voice called from above. We both looked up in surprise. A builder was standing at the top of a ladder rolling paint on the ceiling. 'It's called Thomas Street on the maps, but everyone around here calls it Dysart,' he explained. 'It's just ten miles or so up from Ballinasloe. You'll see it on the great map there.'

There was indeed a Thomas Street north of Ballinasloe. I wondered whether the decorator and I were talking about the same place – how come my grandmother never told me she was born in a town with 'street' in its name? – but we could reach it in half an hour by way of Shannonbridge. There wasn't much detaining us here; clearly Clonmacnoise wasn't going to get any drier.

By law, road signs in Ireland must identify cities and towns by both their English and Irish names except in the Gaeltacht, where they appear in Irish only. Most people find Gaelic signs superfluous outside the Irish-speaking areas; many residents would not be able to spell or even recognise the name of their own town in Irish. But it's government policy and one we approved of as we entered the town. Just below 'Thomas Street' the sign announced that we were entering 'An Deiseirt' – or Dysart. Doubting Thomas had been proven wrong again, this time in Thomas Street.

'Town' is a rather grand word to describe Dysart as it is for many settlements in Ireland, especially in the Irish Midlands. Dysart is essentially a crossing of the roads linking Ballinasloe and Roscommon Town and Athlone with Galway and is surrounded by townland strewn with rocks and stones, earning it the less-than-complimentary nickname 'Stony Dysart'. The centre contains all the requisites of rural Irish life: a church, a couple of pubs and a small shop selling plastic buckets, a few vegetables and stamps. Mike laughed and pointed as we passed the first of the two pubs. The lettering in traditional Gaelic script identified it as 'S. Ó Fallamhain'.

We stopped outside to take photographs of one another below the sign of 'S. Fallon's' and decided we'd return that evening from our B&B in Roscommon Town to gawk and sup inside. It was like a lot of Irish country pubs then, with a turf fire burning in an open hearth, a clay floor, Guinness and Harp pulled from taps and bottles of Paddy's Whiskey on the shelves. Most of the clientele were older men wearing knee-high rubber boots with bits of mud and straw still clinging to their soles and heels. They were talking quietly among themselves and seemed to take little notice of the two new arrivals.

I looked around me and tried to imagine my grandfather in the same pub. Perhaps he'd stood here anxiously pondering the trip by horse cart to Galway the following day and the long and uncomfortable sea voyage to America. The man I never knew beyond his name, a single photograph and a couple of stories passed down, might have leaned against this very bar, wondering whether he'd made the right choice when buying the china dinner service for his bride-to-be on what was his first and last visit home. I had a mixed-up and not-unfamiliar feeling thinking about all these things: this place belonged to a past I shared but it was not part of me at all.

A younger man with a lazy eye and a smile stepped out of one of the groups and approached us, as curious about the two outsiders 'dressed down' in jeans and suede jackets as we were of him and his friends. He introduced himself as Tommy Lynch and asked us our names. 'Oh, another Fallon looking for his roots,' he said with a laugh. 'They're as common as the stars around here, aren't they lads? You'll be wanting to meet my niece. She's my brother's girl from England and knows more about the area than most of us. I'll go and fetch her.'

Though she was born of an English mother and an Irish father, raised in Britain and spoke with a Brummie accent, Bernadette Lynch said she felt more at home in the Irish Midlands than the English equivalent. She was an academic and knew her Irish history as well as she knew Dysart. We arranged to meet the following morning, when she took us on a tour of the area, pointing out the ancient church that local legend said had been destroyed by Cromwell's armies as they raced through Connacht, and knocking on the doors of farmhouses and the church rectory, requesting documents and looking for long-lost relations on my behalf. 'Our ancestors would have known each other,' she said, almost by way of explanation.

I was fascinated by the idea of Bernadette's grandparents and mine having been neighbours, perhaps even friends. We could have been related; we certainly hit it off from the start. The Lynches and the Fallons may have skipped a couple of generations, but here they were back again, doing what they all probably enjoyed most: chatting away, sharing jokes and stories, sipping pints.

Climbing someone else's family tree has all the allure of reading one of those genealogical chapters in the Book of Genesis. It might be of interest to outsiders if the family can find a duke, a poet or a rogue bandit sitting on one of its branches. In general, researching your genealogy is one of the few things in life best done privately.

I caught the bug for a time, not for academic reasons or even out of simple curiosity but with a motive in mind. Armed with my grandparents' names and a few pieces of information I was able to glean in Dysart, I paid visits to the National Archives, the National Library of Ireland and the Public Records Office in Dublin and eventually traced my family and the exact location of the townland where they lived and farmed as far back as the early nineteenth century and, with a few gaps, even to 100 years before that.

The initial return for all my efforts was a standard string of 'begats' – Michael begat Michael who begat Patrick who begat Bernard who begat Thomas who begat Stephen – and documentation that confirmed my ancestors had not been dukes, poets or bandits by any means, but poor indentured farmers. What I didn't know was that until my grandfather's generation and the advent of the national school system for all, they had also been illiterate as evidenced by the self-conscious 'Xs' scrawled above the registrar's insertions and the notations 'his mark' and 'her mark' below.

My reason for all this effort was to secure an Irish passport, a document that would allow me to live almost anywhere in Europe. The Irish government confers citizenship on anyone, regardless of where they were born, who can claim at least one parent or grandparent of Irish birth and I had four of the latter. A passport would be my compensation for enduring all those years of fish on Fridays, Holy Days of Obligation and embarrassing moments in not-so-soundproof confessional booths. For a completed application form, a clutch of documents confirming that – through births and marriages – I was indeed the direct descendant of my grandparents, and a reasonable sum of Irish punts, I received an Irish passport in the mail and henceforth was a bona fide 'citizen of Ireland'.

Official policy and currency on the street can be as different as love and lust. On the dust jacket of Tim Pat Coogan's *Wherever Green is Worn*, a seminal tome about the Irish diaspora around the world, there is a note suggesting that although 'the total population of the island of Ireland is only five million – there are seventy million people on the planet entitled to call themselves Irish'. I'm fairly certain most people in Ireland would disagree with that. With the notable exception of Tim Pat himself, who insisted when I asked him about it that nation or race was an extension of family, the dozens of Irish people to whom I've put the question over the years have always disagreed. An Irish passport doesn't make you Irish, they've said – or words to that effect – and one of them had more than ample authority to make that view unequivocally known.

When we were living in Budapest, I had occasion to call the Irish embassy in Vienna, the closest representation to Hungary at the time. I was trying to jump on the national health insurance bandwagon, hoping my burgundy-coloured European Union/Irish passport with the gold harp on the cover would serve as my *laisser passer* to Ireland's social services.

The attempt was a non-starter as it turned out – I needed to be a resident of the country to qualify – but the receptionist, chatty and full of advice as Irish people so often are, suggested I register with the embassy in the event of an emergency. I'd never bothered doing that anywhere else as a US citizen and I tried to imagine a scenario which would require that my 'compatriots' and I would be spirited away under the cover of darkness by Irish commandos in a jet-propelled speedboat on the Danube. A war maybe? What if I didn't want to leave after all? Suppose I was on the side of the Magyars? Would I have to go?

I gave the woman at the embassy my details and forgot about it until some months later when I received an invitation in the post to attend a reception at one of the big hotels in town. Mary Robinson, Ireland's maverick president who had put the country in a headlock and dragged it into the late twentieth century, was visiting Hungary, and Irish bodies were urgently required.

The function was a relatively small affair; the Irish community in Budapest, or even Hungary, could probably have just about been able to organise a hurling match at the time. As we were assembling, a tall woman entered the room, dutifully announced in Irish by a sergeant at arms – '*An dhaoine uaisle, an tUuachtarán na hÉireann*' ('Ladies and gentlemen, the President of Ireland'). Mrs Robinson leaned over the lectern to make a short address, and when she'd finished, her minder announced that the president would enjoy chatting briefly (five minutes was the imposed limitation) with each of us individually.

'Oh-oh,' I said to my companion, Ruth, an Australian houseguest who was on a Grand Tour of Europe. 'This might be embarrassing.' But Ruth wasn't having any of it. 'Aw, go on,' she said. 'You've got the same passport everyone else does here.'

I was sure that mine had changed colour to a dark blue overnight and that the harp had been transformed into the wing of a golden eagle, but I took my place at the end of the queue and finally approached Mrs Robinson. When she heard my accent, she asked me about my background, what I was doing in Hungary and how I'd come to be at this Irish reception. I told her about the call to the embassy in Vienna. 'I feel like a bit of a phoney,' I began, making a joke about 'my five minutes of shame'. She laughed. It was a full-on, deep-throated laugh that could only make you like her more and wish her well.

I rejoined Ruth and the other guests, and the president returned to the lectern. She summed up Ireland's small but ongoing contributions to the rebirth of democracy in Hungary, the country's nascent economic revival and the cultural exchanges planned. She expressed her thanks to those who were working at an Irish-Hungarian joint-venture dairy somewhere in the south and to the members of VSI, a voluntary organisation. 'And, finally, those of you who have a more tenuous connection with Ireland . . .' she said, looking directly at me and smiling. 'I thank you all for coming this evening.'

A couple of years later, we decided that watching the transformation in Hungary had worn a little thin. The country seemed destined to become 'just another one of those nice little social democratic European republics', as a local travel writer had once told me it would. We moved to London, the self-proclaimed 'coolest city in the world' that rolled up most of its sidewalks when the rest of Europe was just getting ready to step out on the town.

I was in a pub in Islington, North London, one night (no doubt watching the clock closely) when I struck up a conversation with the person standing next to me at the bar. He was a young guy from Limerick, and he didn't look all that well, drawn with dark circles under his eyes and blotches on his neck.

We chatted without any particular purpose except to fill the silence and we covered all the usual London topics: property prices, the weather, cheap flights to destinations on the Continent. When he asked me what part of America I was from – he'd been to Florida, of course, and loved it – I jokingly told him I was Irish too. He didn't seem to think that was very funny. 'You? Irish? You sound like a Yank to me, mate.'

'Well, I am but I've got an Irish passport too,' I said. 'Grandparents and all that.'

He paused for a moment. 'Oh, I'm with you,' he said. 'You'd be another one of those Plastic Paddies then, yeah?'

So, Plastic Paddy – that's what I was. At least it had a name.

London is a peculiar city for Americans to live and work in. Although it looks and sounds familiar – films, songs and nursery rhymes have infused us with place names as diverse as Covent Garden, Notting Hill and Drury Lane and accents as different as Cockney and Kensington – it can also feel even more foreign than places like Hong Kong or Budapest. At least it did to me. Maybe it's because so much is similar on the surface – the language, the Levi's, the McDonald's on every corner – and I wasn't making the same efforts that I would if I were living in a place I considered truly different. But I left London often enough for it to begin to feel like home when I returned and before long Mike and I had settled, buying a house, arranging the furniture, making a life.

Most of the work I was doing by this time involved researching and writing guidebooks, a job that obviously demanded quite a bit of travelling and being away from home. It was a decent enough form of employment, but the lifestyle that went with it was rather unorthodox. I'd go out on the road for a month or two and watch Normandy, County Cork or the Great Hungarian Plain whiz past in a greyish blur, as if I were staring out the window of a high-speed train and was unable to focus on anything but some point in the distance. I'd then return to my desk in London and start climbing the mountain of maps, notes and brochures I'd carried back with me. Once I'd reached the summit and slid down to the bottom, it would be time to start all over again. The road, the blur, the mountain, the slide . . . sure, I learned a fair few things along the way – snatches of languages, aspects of cultures I'd known nothing about, people's aspirations in villages and towns that hadn't changed a great deal in a century – but it could also be as routine as any desk job, any work on any assembly line.

It was a fairly organised work life, too, and had to be with all the deadlines and material collected, the check-in times and lists of things to see and do. I was interviewing a tourist office manager somewhere on the road one morning and ticking off each question as she answered it or handed me more related material. When we'd finished, she leaned back in her chair and smiled. 'Where will you go now that you've crossed us off your list?' she asked nonchalantly. I was embarrassed. I hadn't realised she'd seen me making the Xs in my notebook. What discomfited me more was the thought that she'd come up with a metaphor for my life. I imagined myself as one of those water bugs in a small pond, skimming the surface of the water in a mad frenzy and ignorant of the bottom. Would I ever find out whether it was muck or sand below?

Once in a little country I was doing the same sort of work, roaming from place to place in an organised sort of way, my eyes on the horizon and making ticks and checks whenever something stopped me. There was a voice behind one interruption and a blond-haired, green-eyed smile in front of it. I put my notebook down and followed, staying a lot longer in the little country than any work could demand. Desire had overtaken duty, and it was only when lust began turning to rust that I left the interruption and the little country behind me.

But I'd stayed longer than was wise and damage had been done. I'd never known how easily the moorings can be cut that send us adrift from things and people we love, just how fine the lines are that hold us together. How did I get this far without realising such things? Was I sick the day we learned them at school? Did everyone around me possess a gene that told them these truths instinctively? The wrong person in the right place, the right person in the wrong place. The wrongs and the rights and all their tortuous permutations and combinations had me risk losing something I had considered the most important and constant thing in my life for many years.

'That was a fine summer,' said Mike one night, and I knew he was not referring to the one just past when I'd tarried in the little country. 'That was a good year,' he whispered and looked away. He was talking about a time now past. What had been bound together so tightly for so long had begun to unravel and I wasn't sure how or if I could tie it all back together again.

The past and the present play the key roles in such times, while the future waits for its call on stage. I stopped looking forward and began to question everything current: a fast-paced working life that didn't seem to have a discernible start or finish to it, my relationship with Mike, my disconnection with my family and some of my oldest friends, who seemed to disappear as the well of time and patience ran dry. 'You've changed,' said one and then another, and I knew I'd better find another source to drink from before everything disappeared. This was not their problem but mine.

In a flea market somewhere along the road I picked up a painting on glass of Adam and Eve standing on either side of an apple tree, a snake slithering up the trunk. It wasn't the first one I'd ever bought. I'd collected other such paintings – and woodcarvings and statues too – in the past and placed them all in the corner of a room. A few years had passed since I had added anything to this collection. The future was still firmly on hold. I was travelling backward.

Aunt Alice came to me in a dream one night while I was travelling and I was troubled by it. She looked and sounded downhearted. Alice complained about feeling left out, about having been forgotten. I couldn't imagine the reason for this – she was at centre stage in my memory of childhood and always had been. When I told my sister about the visit and what Alice had said, she wondered whether it had to do with Alice's grave. For one reason or another, we'd never got around to erecting a tombstone over her plot at Cedar Grove Cemetery.

When I returned to Boston on my next visit, my sister and I visited the cemetery where Alice had been buried some fifteen years before. We could locate the site easily enough; it was the one missing tooth in an otherwise perfect row. My sister knew of an old Italian stonecutter in Quincy, and we drove to his workshop to choose a stone.

The stonecutter was alone in his little shop and wanted to talk. I told him about Alice and the missing stone. Like many older people, he seemed to have all the time in the world and I carried on, talking about the Maryknoll mission, the bandages, the Gaelic. We had imagined a marker hewn from local grey granite, with the surface burnished to a brilliant shine. The stonecutter laughed and shook his head. 'They haven't quarried granite here in Quincy for years,' he said. In the end we had to settle for an import – a pinkish stone from North Dakota or some other far-flung place. There just wasn't anything available from close to home.

The old man asked us what we wanted inscribed on the face of the stone. 'With a name like Murphy, you could have something written in Irish,' he suggested. 'That's popular nowadays'. Beyond *céad míle fáilte* and *Erin go bragh* – the hallmarks of Saint Patrick's Day cards and other kitsch, and not exactly what you'd want to put on a gravestone – I couldn't think what we could write. The sign of the cross, the only thing Alice had in the Gaelic, wasn't in the running. This was going to be a gravestone, not a monument atop a massive plinth. About the only extra that would fit was an engraving of the Cross of Saint Bridget with a circle.

Although I'd known for some time that none of my grandparents had been Irish speakers – Alice's version of the Gaelic notwithstanding – I'd assumed that at least their parents, born around the time of the Great Famine, would have had the Gaelic. When I studied the photocopies of their household census return from 1901 that I'd made at the National Archives in Dublin, I discovered the truth about the Irish language and my family's early switch to English. I saw that my great-grandfather and great-grandmother, born in 1846 and 1848 respectively, had been described as speaking 'English only'. A long time had passed since Irish had been part of our world. There didn't seem to be any point in trying to resurrect it now.

The stonecutter's suggestion to include a word or a phrase in Irish stayed with me, and from time to time I thought about peeking into the dark room where I'd left the Gaelic so many years before. I bought a couple of Irish books – one of those 'do-it-yourself' guides that are so badly organised that the vocabulary mentioned in the lessons can never be found in the dictionary at the back –

and a grammar that would have taxed the brain of a rocket scientist. I ducked into them from time to time, but it was pretty crowded and I'd have to come up for air. If vowels are feminine and consonants are masculine, as a poetic phonetician once opined, there was a full house down there. I wondered whether there was any room for me at all.

The idea didn't come to me immediately but when it did it was almost like an epiphany. If I was going backward instead of forward at the moment, I might as well try to learn something new along the way. Something about myself, my family and a language that had been swallowed by the past. More than a century and a half had come and gone since a Fallon – at least our branch of that tree – had spoken Irish. Perhaps I could return to the place where it had once flourished to stop the unravelling and tie a few loose strings back together again for us. It could be an interesting and challenging voyage back to what was once home, and at the very least I might learn how to recite the sign of the cross properly. Aunt Alice would have been pleased.

Chapter IV

Exodus

Countries can look entirely different depending on which side you enter them from. And I'm not just talking about compass points here. Directions have as much to do with memory and the past as they do with maps.

When I'd first visited Ireland decades before, I arrived as a not terribly well-travelled, wide-eyed teenager, and the differences between the old and the new countries were as immediate and shocking as mistaking the cold for the hot tap in a shower on a winter's morning. Cars were being driven on the 'wrong' side of the road, postboxes were an unusual shape and colour, the accents were familiar when I heard individuals speaking but foreign en masse, and everything that looked 'olde worlde' was pretty much that. Take the pubs, for example. They were always full of men in tweed jackets and dunchers, those flat caps that had not been seen in America since Bonnie and Clyde were on the loose and half the country was legless on bootleg.

Now as I walked through the streets of Dublin on a warm July evening a quarter of a century later, it occurred to me that much of what I saw looked commonplace, as familiar to me as everything back in London – from left-hand drive, grocery chains and betting shops on similar high streets to the pubs promising *ceol agus craic* (music and fun) and steadily swallowing thirsty passers-by. Almost everyone I passed looked like a cousin or some distant relation of mine – a curious feeling. I'd always felt more at home among great differences. These similarities were stifling.

I met up with a couple of friends – an Austrian working for the health board (something to do with chemicals in food – I never could get it right and was too embarrassed to ask again) and her Kiwi partner. This being my first night, they suggested we do what everyone does on arrival in the Dirty Old Town: proceed to a convenient public house, down our first pint of 'the black stuff', and, with the single-mindedness of Sisyphus, not quit until the new – and by British standards very generous – closing time of half past twelve. Well, maybe we'd make a pit stop for a bit of blotter along the way, but it would be quick. We were all in agreement on that score. We headed for Mulligan's on Poolbeg Street, a favourite of both locals and tourists anxious to photograph the old-time pub that had appeared in the film *My Left Foot*.

Mulligan's was where I first learned I was going to have company on my voyage of discovery. I was handing Christina her second, pre-poured pint of Guinness when I glanced towards a crowd of people at the lounge bar. A woman was standing at the counter, squeezed uncomfortably between two men and staring at me. 'What's wrong with you?' asked Christina. 'You look like you've just seen a ghost.'

Out of the mouths of babes, I thought. Out of the mouths of babes . . . I said nothing and looked away. When I turned my head back towards the bar again, I could still see her. She had her forefinger pressed up tightly against pursed lips. Very familiar pursed lips, they were. It was Aunt Alice. 'I just thought I saw someone I knew,' I said. 'Over there at the bar.'

'You're always saying that,' Neal laughed. 'How about the time we were at that pub near Hampstead – it was Ryan's birthday, yeah? – and you said you saw a barman you knew from Hong Kong days?'

'True. And I did. He knew me too. He even remembered my name. I didn't remember his though.'

'Yeah, right. And then you said you recognised that waiter at the new Asian place on Upper Street too. Mr Six Degrees of Separation, you. Half of your past must be following you around the globe.'

I suppose it did seem odd. I was always bumping into people I knew in unusual places: an ex-boyfriend from Boston some years later in Paris (he was dating a French priest at the time, of all bejeezin' things); a close childhood friend while I was transiting at Atlanta airport; a Hong Kong television newsreader I'd worked with on a back street in Oxford and then, a decade later, at the Royal Geographical Society in Kensington. Once, in a riverine village in remote Sarawak, we bumped into a friend's next-door neighbour. Of course, all these encounters must have seemed strange, even unlikely, to others. I'd gotten rather used to it.

This was going to be different – I could feel it from the start. As much as I loved and missed everything about Aunt Alice – her laughter and sensible advice along with some of her crazy ways – I sensed trouble. All the others I'd met along the way were temporary, extras in the great double-reel of life, on and off in the blink of an eye. We'd exclaimed greetings, wondered at the incredible coincidence and compared notes. We might even have exchanged addresses. And then we said goodbye. Almost always for good. There must have been a reason why we'd lost contact all those years before. What was the point in starting all over again? With Alice it was different. She was in my thoughts fairly regularly. I just knew it wasn't going to work the same way with Alice.

'Excuse me for a second,' I said and wrung my hands in a gesture signifying an imminent visit to the men's room. Neal and Christina eyed me suspiciously with looks that said, 'Transparent as gin, that one . . .' Men seldom announce their intention to use the toilet; they just get up and go. And everyone knows we don't wash our hands afterwards anyway. At least it got me away from the table, though.

I slipped out the public bar door and hurried over to Tara Street Station. With all the loons and lushes in this town, at least I wouldn't look out of place conversing with the wind if need be. Countless suburban yobbos can be seen doing it nightly as they Dart their way home. I'd fit right in with the crowd.

Alice was by the newsstand at the entrance to the station, scanning the newspapers and magazines with her mouth agape. She was obviously shocked at what she was seeing. I gestured for her to move inside; we'd be on full display otherwise. 'What do you think you're doing here,' I hissed, teeth clenched, eyes slightly menacing. The basic theatricals to imply anger and say 'Go away!'

Alice looked crestfallen and put her head down. She was probably not much older than I was now, and she certainly looked a lot better than when I last saw her on her feet. That was after the heart attack, though, and the arthritis in her hands and a litany of other health problems had left her looking like a rake with big teeth. Now she was wearing an old-fashioned navy blue suit and a funny hat with buttons on it that I recognised from an old photograph I had of her. And, of course, she had on the opened-toed high heels that were her signature footwear. I took the ensemble to be her travelling outfit, and I softened a bit. Clearly she'd planned all this and was trying to look her best for me.

'So, to what do I owe this honour?' I attempted a casual air and a smile, but neither was coming very easily at that moment. She raised her head and glared at me, her eyes flashing. 'I thought you'd asked me to come along!' she almost shouted. 'You were singing "Guardian Angel" the whole way over on the plane!' She sounded defiant and I was beginning to feel dizzy. I always did when women got angry with me, especially Aunt Alice.

As excited as I'd been on the short flight from Heathrow, I'd fallen asleep, the purring of the engine sending me into a dream world where a childhood song I hadn't heard in years reverberated in an empty classroom. The tune and the lyrics had been going through my head ever since, bouncing around like one of those hard rubber balls. In fact, I could still hear it as I stood there facing Alice. 'Oh, come on,' I said, 'that wasn't you. I was just dreaming.'

'Baloney with mustard. Who else would it have been?' Alice began to sing and I wished she wouldn't; the silly song was driving me batty. 'Angel of God, my guardian dear/To whom God's love commits me here/Ever this day be at my side/To light and guard/To rule and guide/Amen.'

I didn't like the sound of this at all, the song and what it implied. The last thing I needed on this journey was some sort of chaperone, a cicerone from the past. Alice had taught me all the Gaelic she knew – thank you very much – and I was counting on doing this thing on my own. That was the point and that was what I'd planned.

'But I've never been here before,' she pouted. 'Everyone else has too.'

This was turning into a plea. I knew what she was referring to. My parents had gone on a tour of Ireland sponsored by Saint Brendan's the summer after I'd graduated from high school. Family word was that Alice had asked if she could accompany them, but my parents told her they preferred to go alone. Maybe they had thought of it as a second honeymoon or just didn't want a relative in tow. I wasn't sure, but no-one deals easily with that sort of rejection. I winced when I thought about how she must have felt.

'And your father travelled with you on your last trip here,' she continued. I looked at her suspiciously. 'You mentioned him in the guidebook,' she said smugly. 'I can still read, you know.' She obviously knew a lot more than I thought she knew, and now she was fighting dirty.

'But it was different when Dad came along . . . ,' I countered but couldn't carry on saying what I was thinking. My father had only appeared from time to time on that trip, mostly just catching a ride when I was driving long distances on my own and I felt like company. I really had invited *him*. He was good company too, making conversation and even offering bits of advice on matters that I had imagined were well after his time. Conversing with the dead; call it prayer. But I couldn't say all that to Alice. It would sound insulting and Alice could be very sensitive.

'Knowing you the way I do, you wouldn't be able to make me leave now anyway,' said Alice. And she was right – we both knew that. Having brought up all that stuff about family and aborted trips to Ireland, she'd be with me for some time to come. Just like that bloody song. I'd never be able to get her out of my mind.

'This is exactly what I don't need,' I mumbled to myself, as I made my way back to Mulligan's and my friends. 'All this family baggage.' I could see steamer trunks, garment bags, hatboxes – you name it – along with my own case, the one full of Irish grammar books and decisions to make.

Dublin did look different – in some ways considerably so – from the way I remembered it from my first visit and not just because of the direction I'd taken to get here this time. Sure, the River Liffey still looked as grimy and viscous as ever, cutting its sluggish way through the centre of town, and the scent of roasted malt filtering over from the Guinness brewery a short distant to the west filled the air as before. But there were building sites at every other corner now, roads to the north and to the south were being ripped open or widened, and the traffic congestion looked as bad as anything in London or Paris. A man sitting next to me on the plane coming over had told me that more cars had been sold in Ireland in the first three months of the year than in all of the previous one. I was already looking at one of the by-products of the country's new-found affluence. And now they were going to build a new metro. Dublin sure had taken on a big city feeling in no time at all.

In Temple Bar, a strip of pedestrian streets, boutiques and music pubs just south of the river, the evening's *craic* was just being kick-started, with groups of young men and women fresh in from Gatwick and Heathrow parading around in silly outfits, determined to make theirs the hen or stag party of the new millennium. Dubliners sitting by the windows of trendy little restaurants, all Med and Asian fusion, minimalist decor and primary colours, looked well-dressed and affluent – the very portraits of the Celtic Tiger lilies gilded in just a few short years.

I couldn't conceive what my grandparents, all of whom had left Ireland on either side of the start of the last century, would have made of all these scenes had they been with me. Those were the days when Ireland did not even rate the moniker 'the sick man of Europe', for a sick man could be made well again. Ireland was the continent's poor, tired old woman or worse. The Irish-language writer Máirtín Ó Cadhain dubbed it 'that dirty old sow which is Ireland'. My grandparents would have thought they'd landed on another planet if they were to see what unfolded before me now. It didn't even bear thinking about.

I crossed Dame Street, dodging the traffic and the roadworks, and popped into The George, Dublin's flagship gay pub. The place wasn't very crowded at this middle hour and the staff easily outnumbered the customers. I sat on a high stool in the corner, staring blankly at the baroque-kitsch decorations and not noticing much around me. But with the ashtrays being changed at every flick of a cigarette, and pint glasses swept away with collars of froth still ringing the bottoms, I soon realised something was out of the ordinary. Almost everyone working the floor was Asian. Chinese, in fact. No other people on earth could be – and perhaps would want to be – that efficient.

'Studying,' a young man from Beijing told me when I asked him what they were all doing and where they'd come from. 'Studying English and making some money.' He smiled. 'Anyway, do you think an Irish person would want to do this job now?' He didn't have time to elaborate. He'd spotted a pint glass about to be drained at the next table and was hovering over it.

The country importing workers instead of dispensing them by the boatload freely (or nearly so) to the rest of the world – that had to be the greatest change of all in the New Ireland. I'd read a newspaper article that morning about a bus driver in Maynooth being prosecuted for making racist remarks to a passenger originally from The Gambia when he'd boarded the bus with a soft drink in hand. There was also an editorial decrying a nation of emigrants denying immigrants. So there had been some fallout over all the new arrivals and no doubt would be even more. Still, I was trying to look on the bright side at the start of my journey. The noodle dishes in Dublin would improve and so would the dim sum. Next thing you knew, there would be Irish fusion food.

Things hadn't changed completely though; you could still find a lot of the Old Ireland in Dublin if you persevered, walked on and kept your head up. Penny whistlers still played their shrill and repetitious tunes along Grafton Street, drunks tried to panhandle the price of a pint from passers-by, and exchanges with shop-keepers and even other pedestrians had all the traditional Irish elements: wit, irreverence, sarcasm.

Earlier in the day I'd been heading for the National Library to climb up the family tree again, when I took a shortcut through Saint Stephen's Green, a lush square of lawn, trees and fountains surrounded by some of the finest Georgian architecture in the city. As the landmark Shelbourne Hotel came into view, a rooster stuck its head out from under a clump of bushes, rustled its brick-red plumage and crowed.

I stopped dead in my tracks; it wasn't something I'd expected to see (or hear, for that matter) in the city centre just opposite one of Dublin's most elegant addresses. My eyes met those of a passer-by just about to enter the green, a sophisticated-looking young woman talking into a mobile phone who wouldn't have been out of place in a provincial city in France. Without missing a step, she pulled the phone away from her ear and addressed me. 'Surely I've heard of him – he's famous,' she told me with a broad grin. 'But I've never actually seen him.' And then, as if sharing a confidence, she whispered: 'I like to think he keeps the nobs at the Shelbourne awake in the morning, don't you?'

Old Ireland was alive and well (if you could call it that) the next morning too when I hopped aboard the Iarnród Éireann train at Heuston Station that would take me to Galway and the west. With the linoleum floors of the vintage carriage covered in cigarette butts, an estimated travel time of almost three hours to cover a distance of just over 200 kilometres and a total of five departures a day from the capital to Ireland's fourth-largest city, 'Irish Ironroad' offered a comfort and service that any Third World country would be proud of. Admittedly, at less than IR£20 one way, it was a cheap ride – at least compared with Britain – but the whole scene reminded me of Poland in the mid-1970s.

The train pulled out of the station and was soon rattling across the midlands, as flat as any potato boxty thrown onto a hot griddle, past grazing sheep, raised bogs and the occasional loch choked with reeds. Once we'd crossed the River Shannon, we were in Connacht, a province with a higher terrain and poorer soil than Leinster, smaller holdings and stone walls that raced along forever with the train.

'To hell or Connacht' was the battle cry of Cromwell's men as they forced 'Papist' farmers off the fertile plains of Leinster and westward, such was their image of this often barren land. I was hoping to find what the poet Oliver St John Gogarthy had called 'A country that is worth the half of Heaven, the whole of Earth'. Connacht was my destination and its Gaeltacht in Connemara was to be home, at least for a while.

Galway on a cold, grey and windy morning in midsummer didn't afford much of a welcome. The streets were heaving with visitors bundled up in jackets; I saw several women wearing woollen scarves and rubbing their hands together frantically as if they'd just deplaned at Anchorage International in December. Most of the tourists were speaking Italian or Spanish. Summer for them meant something quite different from what they were getting in Galway. They probably wondered why they hadn't remained under the sun of Tuscany or Andalucia instead of allowing themselves to be enticed by the cultural centre of the New Ireland.

The smell of the salt air blowing in from the Claddagh and the screeching of the gulls overhead quickly reminded me how easy it was to forgive almost anything of a coastal town – even the crowds and the nasty weather. And I was getting closer to the Gaeltacht and the reason for my journey: to try to learn the Gaelic.

In a minor way, I almost felt as though I had arrived. The city's *Gaillimh le Gaeilge* (Galway with Irish) campaign to encourage public use of the language seemed to have made at least some headway, with shop signs and posters announcing cultural events and even a few advertisements in Irish. I'd never seen Irish used in a modern way – sending out messages about mortgage reductions at a bank, Internet facilities at a café on High Street, postage stamps for sale at a corner shop, a production called *Guth na Mara* (*Voice of the Sea*) at an Irish-language theatre on Middle Street – and wondered how many of these city people could understand the oddly spelled words and complicated sentences.

I made my way to a bicycle shop I knew of around the corner from Eyre Square. If the trains between Dublin and Galway were so infrequent, I wasn't holding out much hope for the bus service in Connemara. The proprietor, Declan, whom I'd met on a previous visit, greeted me like an old friend and asked me what had brought me to Galway again. Was I updating the *Ireland* guidebook so soon? When I told him my plans, he welcomed me all over again but in Irish this time.

'I hadn't realised you were a *Gaeilgeoir* (Irish speaker),' I said. That was something I seldom asked people on previous trips to Ireland. When I did, they'd usually either look embarrassed or would cluck their tongues and roll their eyes, complaining about how they'd had to endure Irish class daily through their school years, just as Poles, Czechs and Hungarians had had to learn Russian before the Wall came tumbling down in Berlin.

Declan explained that, although he'd been born and raised on Oileán Acla (Achill Island), which is officially part of the Gaeltacht in County Mayo, his family spoke English at home. He had learned Irish later when he started working as a fisherman and had continued to speak it only with his colleagues on the job. 'You know, it wasn't until my mates and I were in Germany and we heard another language being spoken all around us that we lost our inhibitions about using Irish together in public,' he said.

He selected a bike for me, and I took it out on the road to test the gears and the brakes. I rode down to the docks and pedalled up Merchants Street back to the shop. A young man in overalls had come in during my absence and was asking Declan something in

Irish about a reconditioned rental bicycle for sale at the front of the shop. Declan asked me if I could understand anything of what he was saying, and the young man switched to English too. Declan gave me a wink that I took to mean 'I told you so' and the visitor walked out, telling Declan he'd come back later. I paid my deposit and left the shop with the bike, feeling like I'd interfered somehow in the normal course of events in a corner of Galway.

I encountered resistance to the language several times as the day wore on. Mary Sexton, who runs what is probably the best B&B west of the Irish Sea, was incredulous when I told her why I'd come to the west of Ireland. 'Learning the Irish?' she'd almost shrieked. 'Now why would you be wanting to do a thing like that? I'd rather fly to the moon than learn the Irish myself!' Her husband, Donal, who had done his early schooling in Irish and could still make conversation, was encouraging, both with my trying to learn the language and the place in which I'd chosen to study it. 'You'll be talking just like them out there in Carraroe when you get back now,' he said with a smile.

Over a plate of *kway teow* noodles at a Malaysian restaurant that evening, I struck up a conversation with the waitress, an attractive young woman and friendly, despite a pouting expression she assumed when her jaws were at rest or she didn't understand something I'd said. She'd arrived from Lorient in Brittany the month before and had just begun working part-time. 'I'm here to learn the language,' she told me when I asked her why she'd come to Galway.

I brightened. Was she in search of ancestral ties? Was she on some sort of pan-Celtic quest? 'Irish? You're here to learn Gaelic?' I asked her excitedly. She looked confused and the pout reappeared. 'No, English,' she said dismissively. 'I think it is enough for me, *n'est-ce pas?*'

The students who had registered for the National University of Ireland summer language program had been instructed to assemble at the Archway, the entrance to an attractive nineteenth-century quadrangle on the campus. There we would board the bus destined for An Cheathrú Rua, the small town called Carraroe in English where the NUI language centre was located. I rode my bicycle the short distance up from where I was staying to the university, locked it and returned to Mrs Sexton's to fetch my bags. Despite all my travelling, I'd never learned the fine art of packing lightly. I always seemed to take too much along with me wherever I went. I never knew when I – or anyone else – was going to need my Swiss Army knife, compass, electric kettle and small library of reading material. It was easy to make friends when you had so much to lend.

My fellow students made for quite a mixed group and we all chatted excitedly without any introductions almost immediately. Predictably, lots of Americans, many of Irish ancestry, were doing the course and they came from a wide range of backgrounds: a professor of classical languages from Berkeley, a singer from an Irish music group in Colorado, a genealogist from Connecticut and a Bible student from Missouri who was as pleased as Punch that he'd just bought a copy of the New Testament in Irish. There were also Germans and Swiss, Catalans and Japanese and even a few Irish people who had lived overseas and managed to elude the years of compulsory Irish tuition required in the national schools.

'Why are you learning Irish?' asked Beth, the singer. 'Are you doing it for credit?' She could have answered the second question herself – I hardly looked like a university student – but she was a delightful person and always trying to please. A clear answer to the initial question escaped me, though. It was the first of many times I'd be asked it and I'd ask it myself of others just as often. I tried to say something about a going backwards, a quest, tying strings together, but it came out all woolly – as it would every time I, and many of the others, attempted a reply. For Beth the reason was more practical: she wanted to perform in Irish and had to learn the language in order to sing it, as opera divas study Italian or German.

The driver was storing our gear in the baggage hold below the coach when I turned to fetch my bicycle and saw that it was missing. I'd unlocked it and leaned it against a railing while I was talking with the others; it was no longer where I'd left it. I ran back into the quadrangle, squinting my eyes and trying to peer into the far corners to see if it had found its way there. In the centre, a group of students in gowns were tossing their mortarboards in the air to celebrate the end of their studies. No bicycle.

'I've lost it before I've even got started,' I thought to myself as I walked through the Archway back towards the bus. This didn't bode well at all. Had Galway become a high-crime area in the New Ireland?

'Are you looking for something?' the bus driver called to me. I could see a dozen quizzical faces pressed against the bus windows just overhead. I told him about my purloined bike. 'But I've already put it down below,' he shouted over the noise of the engine. 'Jump on. We're just about to go.'

We headed south to Salthill, traditionally Galway's seaside playground but now largely an extension of the city, with new tract housing and roundabouts scattered around the low hills. Then we turned west onto the coastal road, passing golf courses, caravan parks and long stretches of sand opening onto the sea. Somewhere around Bearna (Barna), we passed a sign announcing 'An Ghaeltacht'. We were now in the district of Connemara where Irish was – or was supposed to be – the first language of daily intercourse.

Such signs were relatively new, in place less than a decade, and had been opposed by many people, including some in the Irish-speaking districts themselves. They saw no reason to set themselves apart as 'some sort of Indian reservation', as one Irish-speaking Gaeltacht resident told me later, just because they happened to communicate in the 'other' of the nation's two official tongues. In a new, pan-European, more confident Ireland, these signs had become part of the landscape. Now they appeared to be almost a badge of distinction.

I heard some murmurings around the bus. Perhaps the others knew the history behind the signs too. Or maybe they were wondering, as I was, whether English-speaking Ireland and its culture – the only one most of us had ever known or been able to relate to – would look and feel the same after our time in the Gaeltacht.

Conamara (Connemara) is a wild and strange place, a mostly barren patchwork of bogs, mountains, valleys and small lakes and inlets that shimmer when the sun shines. But it's the stone – the grey granite of the boulders covered in pale yellow and green lichen lying everywhere – that is the region's most distinctive feature. While the word 'Connemara' is thought to be a corruption of Conmaicne Mara, the name of the original settlers here, it could just as easily have come from *conamar*, an Irish word meaning 'fragments' or 'broken bits'. With all the rocks and stones strewn about, it's almost as if gods and giant fighting men warred here in some ancient age, leaving massive pieces of broken bone and teeth to petrify in the turf. The stones give the region a forlorn feel, an impression that things can never be put right again.

An Cheathrú Rua is both the name of the first of a series of peninsulas that make up the maze of coastal Connemara and its main town. Some people say 'The Reddish Quarter' owes its name to the soil, which lacks nitrogen and causes vegetation to take on an almost rusty colour. Others say a great fire once engulfed the area, leaving behind a land scorched or *rua*. But *rua* has yet another meaning in Irish: 'wild' or 'fierce'. *Oíche rua* is a 'wild night'. I like to think – in fact, I know – I spent some time in 'The Wild Quarter'.

We arrived at the Áras Mháirtín Uí Chadhain, the NUI language centre named after the writer O'Cadhain, who was born in Connemara in 1907 and is considered among the greatest Irish-language prose writers of the twentieth century. The centre consisted of an older building, a former vocational school built in the 1930s, with offices and classrooms, and a newer structure next to it on a lower level.

We all took seats in one of the larger classrooms and the director, a short, enthusiastic man called Peadar Mac an Iomaire but who would become known to us as Fear Beag Mór (Little Big Man) addressed us in Irish. He said something about the aims of the course and then a word or two (as much as I understood anyway) about speaking only Irish to one another while attending classes at the centre. Then he told an amusing story. Well, it must have been funny; a handful of people in the room were laughing.

'How many of you understood everything I said?' asked Peadar in English. Eight hands went up immediately and he counted them off. 'Very good. You are now the advanced class.

'And how many of you understood nothing?' I froze. It wasn't exactly nothing I understood, but there certainly was a lot that I didn't grasp. I kept my hands on the desk. 'Okay, that's, umm, ten, eleven, twelve. You're all in the beginners' class,' said Peadar. 'As for everyone else, you will make up the *meánrang*.'

Oh-oh. Of the fifteen of us now making up the 'intermediate level', almost everyone had done at least a year of Irish in some sort of classroom situation; several of them had done courses at the university level. The genealogist had already done the beginners' course twice at the centre. I was the odd one out for sure.

Okay, I'd done a little preparatory work beforehand, flipping through the pages of my DIY language book and listening to the tape so I guess I could say I knew something about how the language worked, as convoluted and vowel-saturated as it looked. But I'd just been surfing; I didn't even know how to pronounce most of the words I saw on the wall posters and the book spines on the shelves – much less how to decline even a regular verb. What had I been thinking? Size does matter when it comes to learning a language, and the *meánrang* was going to be a pretty large class, especially for someone as ill-prepared as me. What sort of teacher could rein in such a motley bunch with so many levels of experience and so many different reasons for learning the language?

There was no time to concern myself with all that just then. We'd soon be going into our first class – on Saturday – and all my questions would surely be answered. As we'd all learn quick enough, there would be no messing about in An Cheathrú Rua that summer, at least where learning the Irish language was involved.

We settled into the homes of our various host families quickly and without a hitch. In fact, when I look back on it all now, it seems surprising just how smoothly the transition took place at the beginning. Perhaps the goal of learning at least some Irish – however fuzzy the motivation – and the fact that we were now in the language's epicentre helped us to overlook all the little disappointments and minor details and just get on with it.

Maybe it was easy because the homes and their families felt so familiar: the overstuffed armchairs in the living rooms; the kitchens where everyone would congregate to gossip and exchange stories over endless cups of tea; the statues of Saint Antony of Padua turned towards the wall, suggesting that someone had misplaced something important yet again; and the three square meals daily of meat, meat and more meat cooked to varying shades of grey and served with boiled potatoes and stewed vegetables. That was just the way my mother used to prepare our meals in the 1950s and 1960s, when no self-respecting Irish-American housewife kept garlic in the pantry and paprika was considered racy. I felt at home immediately.

The house of the family I'd been assigned to was a relatively new, L-shaped structure facing the main road in Doire Fhatharta Mór (O'Flaherty's Great Wood), a treeless townland just a couple of kilometres north of the town's centre. The family and the lodgers stayed in the sprawling main building. Next to it was a smaller structure from which they ran a used furniture store. From the mansard window in my rooftop room I could look across the

53

fields and ancient stone walls to Loch an Mhuilinn (Mill Lake). Beyond it was Cuan Chasla (Cashla Bay) from where the boats sailed to the Oileáin Árann, the three windswept Aran Islands in Galway Bay and bastions of the Irish language.

Four other students were also staying in the house: Marsha, a very graceful professional dancer from somewhere in New England; Paul, a copywriter from New Jersey who was obsessed by the Gaelic and by Irish music; Marcus, a male nurse from Germany; and Jen, a student from Pennsylvania, who from the start conversed easily in Irish with Bríd, the *bean an tí*, or 'lady of the house'. Bridey, as she preferred to be called, had been born and raised in an older house just a few doors down the road and was thus a true native of An Cheathrú Rua. Her husband, the *fear an tí*, Seán, hailed from the Ceantar na nOileán (Islands District) to the west. They had four children.

The family would speak to us in a mixture of the two languages, pronouncing each word of Irish clearly but never slowly or in a loud voice as many people do when speaking to foreigners as if they were talking to dimwits or someone hard of hearing. '*Cleachtadh, cleachtadh anois*,' Bridey would encourage me regularly to 'Practise, now practise', and I'd repeat a phrase or – shudder – try to form a whole sentence from the small bank of words at my disposal. Those of us with a lower level of Irish would often lapse into English. We may have been cheating, but we felt comfortable in such a bilingual house, without having to perform all the time or feel left out if the conversation drifted away from the weather or what we wanted for lunch the next day. If language's primary purpose was communication, we were certainly achieving that and it created an atmosphere of camaraderie. We all felt part of the family in no time.

Seán liked to tell a story, something he excelled at, and on our first night, after we'd finished dinner and started on our second pot of tea, he talked a little about his childhood in the Islands District. He had been born and raised on one of the smaller islands in the archipelago, some of which were linked by a bridge or a causeway. His island had neither; going to the mainland or another island meant rowing the *currach*. The island also lacked electricity and a secondary school, so when he'd finished primary school Seán and some of the other children from the district were shipped off to a state-run boarding school in Dublin to finish their education. I asked him whether he enjoyed his time in the big city and he shook his head at once. 'It was the worst two years of my life,' he said. 'I had but two words of English at the time – "yes" and "no". Those Dublin lads gave us hell.'

'But didn't they think you were special – speaking Irish and all?' asked Jen. She was an intelligent young woman, an anthropology student at Cornell, but at her age was not one with a particularly long memory.

Seán looked somewhat baffled and then grinned. He would have heard all the talk about Irish being considered trendy among certain Dublin youth, perhaps had visited one of the Irish-speaking café-restaurants in the capital and seen the activist T-shirts with sentences like *Tír gan teanga, tír gan anam* (A country without a language is a country without a soul) written on them. The recent arrival of Irish-language television, with some cutting-edge programming and a couple of cult personalities and heart-throbs whose names were constantly in the national press and on everybody's lips, would have helped to sow those seeds.

'It was a different time then,' said Seán, looking a little sad. That would still have been the era when English-speaking Ireland regarded Irish not only as a drudge to have to suffer daily at school but also as the language of yokels and country bumpkins – a despised symbol of poverty, backwardness and emigration. English was the language of education, employment and advancement; Irish was the mother tongue of the 'dirty old sow'.

I asked Seán whether he felt more Irish than his fellow citizens in the Galltacht, the English-speaking districts of Ireland and basically the entire country. They might be able to rustle up *cúpla focal*, 'a few words', remembered from schooldays if need be when visiting the Gaeltacht or making a speech in an official capacity, but lived their lives and dreamed their dreams exclusively in English. He shook his head. 'Oh, not at all,' he said. 'I guess we're just happy to still have the Irish,' he said. Why would people feel proud of something so much a part of their lives just because others had decided it was now fashionable?

Outside in the driveway Paul was teaching the couple's two younger sons how to play softball. He'd instruct them in Irish as best he could – Paul's Irish was strong but 'softball', 'foul' and 'strike' may not have reached the Gaelic lexicon yet – and the boys would dutifully respond. When they did foul, walk, strike out or call to the dog Fluffy not to get too close to the road, they shouted in English. Perhaps Irish wasn't the language for anger or fear but for songs, stories and memory.

Our first class was, gratefully, an abridged one and we were out the door by lunchtime. 'That was a fine section of the road to hell paved,' said Anne, a young Canadian woman with raven hair who taught Irish history at the university in Galway. I had to agree; we'd learned a lot in a couple of short hours. Even so I continued to wonder whether I'd bitten off more than I could possibly get my tongue around. Irish was going to be tough – that much was clear. With thoughts of imminent self-demotion on my mind, I hopped on the bicycle to explore something of my new surroundings. I'd heard the peninsula was famous for its fine beaches, particularly one called Trá Choiréalach (Coral Beach) that was a strand composed entirely of coral-like fragments, and I was anxious to have a look.

I rode south, past the town centre, and then headed west. The road was flanked by nondescript houses built with breeze block and then faced with tile – no whitewashed stone cottages, no thatch, no turf smoke curling lazily out of a rickety old chimney. An Cheathrú Rua was essentially a new town. Most of the homes I passed on the road to the beach looked as though they had been built when a book called *Bungalow Bliss* took Ireland by storm in the late 1970s. It contained plans for dozens of houses like these. The residents of An Cheathrú Rua must have bought up a large part of the first print-run.

The peninsula did have a past. There were holy wells, sacred streams and famine graves marked everywhere on the map that I was using. One of the older stone buildings had been the site of a skirmish during the so-called Land Wars in 1880. Hundreds of local people had tried to prevent the eviction of tenants by an absentee landlord; dozens of constables were called in and one person was killed and several wounded in the ensuing struggle. It was funny to imagine what this place would be like if the leaders of the 1916 Uprising had been called O'Lenin and MacTrotsky and Ireland had followed the road to communism. An Cheathrú Rua would have become a centre of national homage, the rioters raised to the status of revolutionary heroes and the old slate-roofed building a pilgrimage site for Young Pioneers.

The last stretch of road led me through a sentry line of conifers, quite a find in this treeless landscape, and down a steep hill, which offered a bit of cool relief in the heat of the afternoon sun. At the bottom, fanning out northward, was the beach, small patches of coarse sand punctuated by sharp rocks, with a thick lip of seaweed at the edge. I didn't like the idea of wading through all that wrack but the sea, an iridescent blue and much warmer to the touch than I'd expected, was irresistible. I'd put a bathing suit in my knapsack before I'd set out, never really thinking I'd make much use of it, and there was a changing room attached to the public toilets just where I'd left the bike.

The sea air felt chilly when I climbed out of the water so I raced up and down the beach, the sand squeaking at every footfall, to warm up. The small hill overlooking the beach was bathed in sun so I climbed up and lay down, reaching for my notes from class. We were indeed learning intensively – we'd already covered the first four of some three dozen lessons in the text – and I decided I'd better try to keep pace if I was to make a go of it, whatever level I found myself in.

Cá bhfuil mé? (Where am I?) . . . *Cá bhfuil tú?* (Where are you?) . . . *Cé hé tusa?* (Who are you?) . . . *Cé hé mise?* (Who am I?) I knew the questions but not the answers just yet, so I tried hard to concentrate on reviewing what we'd learned and trying not to look ahead. But every time I started at the top of the page to repeat the sample sentences and new vocabulary, my eyes would stray across the yellow gorse and purple heather covering the hillside and down to the water, a narrow section of what they called Cuan an Fhir Mhóir (Bay of the Great Man). Who was that Great Man? A powerful famine landlord long since forgotten or someone who truly deserved the moniker?

I thought of that past Easter in Paris with Mike and the good times we'd had despite all the rain, and the one before in Amsterdam to celebrate his birthday and all the fog that blocked the view of the canal from the hotel we'd chosen to stay at. It didn't seem to make much difference then. I tried to imagine where the next one would find me or him or us, and how the weather would be at the time.

Close to the opposite shore of Oileán Garomna (Gorumna Island) a *húca*, a boat called a hooker in English with a pitched black hull and russet-coloured sails, once common to the area, was making its way rapidly southward in a stiff breeze. The sails reminded me of a junk we'd gone scuba diving from in Hong Kong, and I travelled there for a while too, remembering the small octopus that had sprayed ink at us when we swam after it, causing us to lose our way for a time. Then, as we returned, we sailed right into a late summer typhoon that blew us around the South China Sea as though we were sitting in the bottom of a walnut shell floating in a bathtub. It had been as if some Great Man was playing with us, a cat amusing itself with an injured mouse, flipping us into the air and landing us with a great thud on the troughs of the waves. I'd driven a long splinter under my fingernail when I'd grabbed the mast to steady us both, and I winced remembering the wave of pain I felt shooting up my arm.

I reached into my bag for my mobile phone but no signal registered when I turned it on. I leaned back and closed my eyes and must have dozed off for a while. I didn't dream, but I heard music – singing – which sounded like it was coming from above.

> Sure, a little bit of heaven fell from out
>   the sky one day
> And it nestled on the ocean in a spot
>   so far away
> And when the angels found it, sure it
>   looked so sweet and fair
> They said, 'Suppose we leave it for it
>   looks so peaceful there?'
> So they sprinkled it with stardust just
>   to make the shamrocks grow
> 'Tis the only place you'll find them no
>   matter where you go
> Then they dotted it with silver to make
>   its lakes so grand
> And when they had it finished, sure
>   they called it Ireland.

Alice. I opened my eyes and looked up the hill. She was sitting on a rock, looking out to sea. She looked different, younger maybe, and was dressed in a light cotton blouse and a pair of sporty Bermuda shorts that I might have remembered from a summer cookout decades before, or perhaps from a photograph. It was hard to tell. I noticed she'd changed the stilettos for open-toed espadrilles.

'Oh, Al, is this how you're going to make your grand entrance every time you visit?' I teased her. 'Filling up my head with all those corny songs that will never go away?'

Alice ignored the question and glanced around her with a slight frown on her face. I wondered whether she was still annoyed with me for my less-than-enthusiastic welcome in Dublin two nights before.

'It doesn't look anything like I thought it would,' she said, almost whispering it to herself. 'All this awful grey stone . . . Where are the forty shades of green?'

Hers wasn't the first such reaction I'd heard about this land-scape; Connemara is one of those places that people either can't leave or can't wait to get away from. My mother was definitely in the second camp. Once on a trip we'd taken together a decade before, we'd passed through this area on our way to Carna and points beyond. She disliked it so much she burst into tears and pleaded for us to move on quickly; this melancholy land was not the Ireland of her imagination. Perhaps Alice would have preferred the gentler countryside down in Cork or Kerry, counties with all the familiar Irish-American icons and pilgrimage sites: Blarney Castle, the Ring of Kerry, the *Ryan's Daughter* film locations. They were places I wanted to visit once too, when I was entering Ireland from the other side.

'It's a small place, isn't it?' she continued. 'Everybody will be knowing each other's business here, I'd say.' Alice had always kept pretty much to herself on Sedalia Road, greeting neighbours in a friendly way but staying apart somehow. I used to think she was being snobby. Everyone in her neighbourhood – down Sedalia Road, up Elmer Road, along Burgoyne Street – was Irish and some of them had moved over from Southie, a much rougher Irish neighbourhood than her part of Dorchester. Maybe she felt superior to them.

It wasn't until later that I realised there was a reason: you don't get any more say in picking your neighbours than you do in choosing your family, but your family will always be your family, she'd said. Alice was very family-orientated, and she and her five siblings had been raised to take care of one another. That would have come from her mother, a strong, even dominating, woman who had emigrated to America first and then sent for the rest of her family in Ireland one by one. Different times, different ways. Sometimes I wasn't sure where my family was, physically or mentally, and they must have felt the same about me.

Now I was beginning to wonder just which 'small place' Alice had been talking about. An Cheathrú Rua? Connemara? The whole country of Ireland?

'There's an old graveyard beyond the changing room at the bottom of that hill you rode down,' she said, before I had a chance to open my mouth, and pointed. I'd read about that in a guidebook to Connemara I'd bought in Galway. A children's burial ground dating from the Famine. Opposite it was a beach called Trá na bPáistí. That was a funny thing – naming a beach after a cemetery full of dead kids. 'You can avoid it by walking your bike along the sand and listening to the sound of the surf,' she said.

I tried to get my mind around the lessons again, but the sun had shifted by then and the sweatshirt I'd brought along wasn't heavy enough to keep the sea breeze out even on a July afternoon. I jumped back onto the bike and headed for the road back to town, not dragging the bike along the sand but staying as far to the right as was legal.

The bike and I had a tough time battling our way up the hill against the wind and I was panting by the time I'd reached the top. As I approached the town I decided I'd earned my first pint of Guinness *as Gaeilge* (in Irish). Just on the left was a place called An Réalta with a pub sign displaying a large, five-pointed star.

'The Star' had few windows and I stood at the entrance waiting for my eyes to adjust to the shadowy interior after the light of a summer afternoon. The barmaid smiled and greeted me in English though I'd attempted to do the same in Irish. Strike one. She pulled me a pint of Guinness but it tasted oddly sour, as if someone had squeezed a wedge or two of lemon in the glass before filling it. When I looked around I saw that almost everyone else in the room was drinking beer or lager. I obviously didn't know my way around yet.

On the last stretch before the town centre, I could see something lying in the middle of the road up ahead and I squeezed the handbrakes as tightly as I could, almost flipping over the handlebars. It was a body. I glanced around in panic and saw an old man sitting on a stone wall on the edge of the pavement, a walking stick tucked between his legs.

'*Dia duit*,' he said, or 'God with you', the somewhat exclusionary but most common greeting in Irish. I looked at the body again – I could see it was a young man now – and then anxiously back at the old man. He made a gesture of putting a glass to his mouth and grinned.

The young man was dead drunk and lying face down on the road, his teeth practically embedded in the asphalt. I approached him and tried to rouse him by tugging on his arm, but he was almost unconscious. I started to shout at him but wondered what I should say; lessons one through four had got me questioning where and who I was but hadn't offered any help in rousing drunks sleeping in the centre of a country road. I supposed I could manage to ask him if he was okay. '*An bhfuil tú ceart go leor?*' I stammered. That was a mouthful.

Rip O'Winkle mumbled something unintelligible – to me anyway – and remained 'in his lying'. I should at least move him closer to the curb, I thought, and tried dragging him over towards the pavement. I was still pulling on this dead weight, covering very little ground in the process, when a car came to an abrupt stop on the opposite side of the road. A woman jumped out. '*A Dhiarmaid!*' she shouted and raced over to the man whose name I had just learned was Dermot. She looked at me and assuming I was a tourist, a blow-in or some other form of *eachtrannach* (foreigner), spoke to me in English. 'Just look at the state of him,' she said with disgust. 'I'll be taking him home now.'

The woman had apparently had practice dealing with young Dermot in this state before. In a flash she had brought him to his feet, shouldered him over to the car and pushed him into the front seat. The old man and I watched the car drive off. Irish womanhood in control, Irish manhood out of control and everyone else watching from the sidelines. Not everything had changed in the New Ireland.

When I got back to the house, Paul and the young boys were engaged in a boisterous, bilingual game of Crazy Eights on the floor of the sitting room, and Marsha was helping Bridey with the tea in the kitchen. Seán was out front unloading some furniture from a lorry that had just arrived from Britain. He only stocked British goods, he'd told me the night before, and when I asked him why he'd said that local people would never buy used Irish furniture. The new confidence in all things Irish hadn't filtered down to settees and three-piece suites, at least in these parts.

'*A Stiofáin*,' he greeted me, and sat on one of the wooden chairs he'd just removed from the truck. 'How did you find the Réalta?' he asked. 'It won't get going till after dinnertime.'

His question took me by surprise. 'You weren't in The Star, were you?' I asked him. I'd only seen a couple of old boys in the front room and some lads playing snooker in the back. Seán hadn't been with either group.

He grinned and offered me a cigarette. We smoked the same brand, which we'd both decided was very convenient in a little place where all-night corner shops were at a premium. 'Shame about yer man, Dermot, ya know? Too young to be on the drink like that.'

Alice had been right. I'd arrived in a small town in a small part of a small country. I had better watch my step, in any language. 'Was there a match on this afternoon?' I asked. 'Maybe his team won.' Or lost. I was trying to think of a reason for young Dermot's over-indulgence and his choice of bed. Who knew what defences I myself might need to lay down in future?

Seán shrugged and picked up a couple of chairs. 'Any excuse here,' he called out over his shoulder and disappeared into the store.

Chapter V

The Gaelic

The language I'd come to Connemara to study is called Irish, though many people in the diaspora continue to use its older name, Gaelic (pronounced '*gay*-lic'), as Alice did. The reasons for this habit are based in history. The word Gaelic was in common use in the mid- and late nineteenth century during the so-called Gaelic Revival, when efforts were first made to breathe new life into the language. This was the time when the ancestors of many overseas Irish, including mine, emigrated and the term persisted.

'Gaelic' is closely related to *Gaeilge*, the Irish name for the language, but it is rarely heard in Ireland today. About the only people who use it are the very old and academics trying to 'reclaim' the term in order to make a clearer distinction between, say, Irish literature in the English language – works by James Joyce, William Butler Yeats and Samuel Beckett – and writings in Gaelic.

The history of the Irish language is a long and tortuous one, full of plots and subplots. It is an epic story of battles won and lost, of victories and failures, and one in which words like 'birth' and 'death', 'revival' and 'obituary' loom large. Though often employed for reasons of political or personal gain and thus used inaccurately, these metaphors can help to understand where Irish is coming from, where it is now and where it is going.

Irish is a Celtic language, of which three others are still spoken. Scottish Gaelic (pronounced '*gal*-lic') and Welsh have approximately 80,000 and 500,000 speakers in Britain respectively. Breton, in France's westernmost province of Brittany, counts more than 700,000 but only a quarter of them speak it regularly.

Scottish Gaelic (*Gàidhlig*) and Irish are closely related; in fact, the dialect of Irish spoken in Donegal can be understood relatively easily by a native speaker in the Western Isles of Scotland. Welsh (*Cymraeg*) and Breton (*Brezhoneg*) are cousins, though not mutually intelligible with Scottish Gaelic and Irish. Other Celtic languages once spoken in the British Isles but now extinct as a first language include Cornish (*Kernewek*), a variant of Welsh used in Cornwall until the late eighteenth century, and Manx (*Gailck*), which is spoken by a few people in the Isle of Man who learned it as a second language. The last native speaker of Manx died in 1974.

The early history of the people known as the Celts is murky, but it is thought that they originated somewhere in the eastern part of central Europe around the second millennium BC and began to migrate across the Continent. Archaeological finds from Hallstatt near Salzburg in Austria indicate that a Celtic Iron Age culture, one of the first in Europe, lived there as early as 800 BC. The decorative S shapes, spirals and circles in the metalwork of the later La Tène culture found near Lake Neuchâtel in Switzerland are the same as those unearthed in Ireland.

The early Celts were an excitable, ferocious and warlike people who, according to the first century BC historian Diodorus Siculus, were tall in stature, bleached their hair white and wore bronze helmets and brightly coloured cloaks fastened at the shoulder with large brooches. They were much feared by the Greeks and the Romans, who called them the Keltoi or Gallatae, both variations of words for 'barbarian'. They lay siege to Rome for several months in 390 BC and eventually reached as far east as the Black Sea and Anatolia in Turkey and as far west as northern Spain and the British Isles. The tribes split into various groups – Celto-Iberians in Spain, Gauls in France, Galatians in Anatolia – and developed variations of their own languages and cultures.

By the first century BC the Celtic groups had been subdued by Rome and their wanderings came to an end. Most assimilated with their neighbours, and their language – Common Celtic – disappeared by the start of the Christian era, replaced for the most part by Latin. Those who went farther afield, crossing the English Channel and the Celtic Sea to the British Isles, retained their language. It was this 'Insular Celtic' and its variations that would survive to a greater or lesser degree as the Celtic languages still spoken today.

These island Celts crossed over from Gaul to Britain and Ireland sometime between 500 and 300 BC and their language, called Goildelic (from the Old Irish word *Goídel*, meaning 'Celt'), began to develop independently, making it one of the oldest languages in Europe. With the decline of Roman rule in Britain at the start of the fifth century, settlers from Ireland introduced the language along the west coast where it took hold in Scotland and the Isle of Man and eventually developed into Scottish Gaelic and Manx. In Wales and Cornwall, Brythonic, the forerunner of Welsh and Cornish, remained the dominant language among British Celts. Displaced by the Anglo-Saxon invasions in the fifth and sixth centuries, Celts from Cornwall established a colony in Brittany, and Breton eventually emerged as an independent Celtic language.

In Ireland, storytelling and other oral traditions were, from earliest times, the domain of *file*, poets or bards with magical powers who kept history, legend and ritual alive. Around AD 400 a primitive form of writing called 'ogham' appeared. It employed a variety of strokes and notches cut above, below or across a keyline on the edges of stone pillars or posts. These ogham standing stones, examples of which can still be found in the counties of Kerry, Cork and Waterford, served as grave markers or homilies extolling the virtues and feats of local kings or chieftains.

Christian missionaries from Britain and Gaul, with Saint Patrick in the vanguard as early as the fifth century, introduced the Latin alphabet to Ireland. Monks made adaptations to accommodate Irish sounds not represented by the new script, and writing in the language now known as Old Irish began to appear some time in the late seventh century.

In the beginning, writings in Irish were mostly religious tracts, elegies and verse – Ireland's reputation as an 'island of saints and scholars' was established early on – but before long scholars and scribes began to commit histories, epics and sagas dating from much earlier periods to writing. These included such tales as *Táin Bó Cúailnge* (*The Cattle Raid of Cooley*), with its boy warrior Cú Chulainn, and the bloody *Scéla Mucce Meic Dathó* (*Tale of Mac Dathó's Pig*), which describe in gory detail life in the Ireland of the first and second centuries AD. Some wonderful verse also appeared at this time. An anonymous poet's ode to his cat named Pangur Bán (White Pangur) is still as fresh and contemporary as it was when written some 1200 years ago. Vernacular Irish literature can thus be counted among the oldest in Europe. By contrast, the Old English epic *Beowulf* appeared in written form some time around the end of the first millennium.

The role of the Irish monasteries, which developed in the sixth and seventh centuries and did not always fit the pattern prescribed by Rome, was instrumental in safeguarding the literary traditions of the Irish language. During this 'Golden Age', Ireland was the only Western European country whose vernacular was considered suitable for education and literature. By the eighth century, Irish had largely replaced Latin as a religious medium and was cultivated by the monastic orders. In effect the monks became the publishers of Europe and their missionaries spread Christianity and learning throughout Europe, particularly among the Celts' original neighbours, the Germanic tribes. But invasions by the Vikings from the north, starting in the late eighth century and continuing for more than 200 years, disrupted the monastic system, and the role of literary guardian passed from the monks to secular writers and hereditary bards.

The bards, who trained for seven years and relied on noble patrons for support, wrote in a bastardised form of Old Irish now known as Middle Irish that was much closer to the everyday spoken language. Many of the poems had religious themes or were syco-phantic paeans to the bards' patrons; verse expressing courtly love would have to await the arrival of the Anglo-Normans in the twelfth century. Popular stories about various *fiana* (war bands) found their way into what is called the Fenian cycle of tales and ballads, which focuses on the life and deeds of the hero Fionn Mac Cumhaill (Finn Mac Cool). These folk tales remain some of the most popular in Ireland today and are still read by children.

The Vikings established towns along the coast, including Dublin, and for some time remained in control of Ireland's trade and commerce. In 1014, however, they were defeated by the Irish high king, Brian Boru, at the Battle of Clontarf on the shores of Dublin Bay. Most of the Scandinavians were absorbed into the local culture, and their language had little influence on Irish except for a handful of seafaring and fishing terms and common words such as *beoir* (beer), *lochta* (loft) and *fuinneog* (window) that are still used in Irish today.

While the kings of the provinces of Munster, Connacht, Leinster and Ulster jockeyed for dominance over the next century, Gaelic Ireland remained independent. In hindsight, the disruptions caused by the Vikings would seem almost benign compared with what was to come.

In the middle of the twelfth century the king of Leinster, Diarmait Mac Murchada, promised his inheritance to an Anglo-Norman adventurer called Richard de Clare, the Earl of Pembroke and bet-ter known to history as Strongbow, if he would send forces to subdue Mac Murchada's royal rival, the king of Connacht. In 1169 Strongbow did just that and, with the death of Mac Murchada two years later, became king himself.

Henry II, the first of England's Norman kings, had been named 'lord of Ireland' by the pope in a bid to further church reform across the Irish Sea. He grew concerned that the independent-minded Strongbow might use his power base in Ireland to recoup lands denied him in England. In 1171 Henry sailed to Waterford with a large naval force and declared it a royal city.

The Anglo-Norman invasion had in effect brought an end to the real independence of Gaelic Ireland and set the stage for more than 800 years of English (and later British) involvement. The story of the Irish language – both its demise and revival – would be inextricably linked with that of English from this time onward.

To lay all the blame on the English for the next eight centuries of subjugation and oppression is tempting but facile; like most relationships, the association of the English and Irish languages was, and remains, a lot more complicated than that. From the start there were apologists and rabble-rousers. The chronicler Giraldus Cambrensis (Gerald of Wales) was among the first to heap scorn on the Irish, their culture and their language in his *Topography of Ireland* in 1188. This diatribe would be quoted again and again in the next several centuries to underscore the inferiority of all things Irish. But the colonised can acquiesce to the coloniser and, for reasons of economics, expediency or ambition, will sometimes carry the banner even higher themselves. The willingness of the population to contribute to the spread of English over Irish is surely one of the reasons the language shift occurred so rapidly in Ireland.

The effects of the Anglo-Norman invasion were not felt in Ireland immediately. For at least the first century or so, the new barons from across the sea continued to speak their own language – Norman French – and it became the medium of commerce, government and the law. By the time England lost control of the duchy of Normandy in the thirteenth century, English had begun to emerge as the language of the towns in Ireland. The rest of the country, however, continued to speak Irish.

The Gaelic chieftains soon recovered a substantial amount of territory from the invaders, and there was a resurgence, even a flowering, of Irish culture. The invasion had been something of a leveller for the spoken language, and the Irish literati undertook a new standardisation of the written language. By about the year 1200 an early form of Modern Irish, called Classical Irish, emerged in both the written and spoken form; it would remain the literary standard not only in Ireland but in Gaelic Scotland and on the Isle of Man until as late as the seventeenth century.

Equally important, many of the Anglo-Normans had begun to assimilate with the local population, adopting the language and Irish customs and often becoming 'more Irish than the Irish themselves', as one contemporary chronicler put it. The Anglo-Normans contributed a number of words to the Irish language, including *gasúr* ('boy' or 'child' from *garçon*), as well as the prefix 'Fitz' in names like Fitzgerald or Fitzpatrick, which was derived from the Norman French *fils* (son).

The Gaelicisation of the Anglo-Norman population in Ireland greatly concerned the English Crown, and the king was determined to rein in what he expected to be his loyal subjects. In 1366, England promulgated the Statute of Kilkenny. It proscribed (ironically, in Norman French) the use of the Irish language – as well as 'alliance by marriage . . . or by amour' with Irish people – among all *Englishmen* living in the 'obedient' lands (that is, those controlled by England). These lands, including Dublin, Wexford and Waterford, would later become known as the Pale. The population outside the limits of these areas, rural-based and overwhelmingly Irish-speaking, was left pretty much to its own devices. They were governed by the Brehon Law, the local Irish code that the statute dismissed as one that 'reasonably ought not to be called law, being a bad custom'.

The Tudors, who ascended to the throne in 1485, were responsible for consolidating and extending English rule in Ireland; the Irish Parliament declared Henry VIII king of Ireland in 1541. But despite a series of acts enjoining that English, and only English, be the medium of communication within the Pale, the Crown was ambivalent toward the Irish language elsewhere in the country.

Henry's break with Rome, and the Act of Supremacy confirming him as head of the Church both in England and Ireland, complicated matters tremendously since one of the principles of the Reformation was the preaching of the Gospel not in Latin but in the language of the people. As directives were issued under Henry's daughter, Elizabeth I, setting out who must speak English in Ireland and where, the first book printed in the Irish language in Ireland – *Aibidil Gaoidheilge agus Caiticiosm* (*Gaelic Alphabet and Catechism*) – appeared in 1570 as an aid in converting the 'Papists' to Protestantism.

Elizabeth provided type and press for the first Irish translation of the approved *New Testament*, which was published in 1602, and was the force behind the establishment of Trinity College founded in 1591 in Dublin for the propagation of the Protestant faith. She personally expressed an interest in learning the rudiments of the Irish language. A phrasebook in Irish, English and Latin was dutifully readied for her around 1585. Whether she ever made use of it is unknown.

The last year of Elizabeth's reign would prove to be a watershed in the history of Ireland and, by extension, the Irish language. By the turn of the seventeenth century, England had reduced most of the Anglo-Irish earls and the Gaelic and assimilated Anglo-Norman population in the provinces to obedience. Just one holdout remained – the province of Ulster – and the Crown had been fighting a protracted war with its chief, Hugh O'Neill, since 1594. That came to an end in 1601 when the English defeated a combined force of Ulstermen and Spaniards in the Battle of Kinsale, south of Cork. O'Neill made it back to the north but surrendered shortly after the queen's death two years later. In 1607 he and ninety other Ulster earls sailed for Catholic Europe, never to return. Gaelic civilisation at the upper levels of society had been completely destroyed.

The so-called Flight of the Earls left Ulster – the last outpost of

71

independent Gaelic Ireland – without a leader. Elizabeth's successor, James I, implemented a program of colonisation called plantation that had first been attempted without success in Munster and Leinster by Elizabeth and her sister and predecessor, Mary. The 'Great Plantation' was an altogether different story, and large numbers of settlers were lured to Ulster with the promise of land.

Unlike the Vikings and the Anglo-Normans, the new invaders – a large proportion of them English-speaking Protestants from Scotland – did not intermarry and kept very much to themselves, not assimilating at all. The hills and lowland bogs went to local Irish and 'Old English' (Anglo-Norman) Catholic tenant farmers, causing resentment and anger that sowed the seeds of rancour and hostility that continue to divide Ulster today.

The seventeenth century was one of conflict that closed with Gaelic Ireland even more disenfranchised than it had been at the start, and the position of the Irish language weakened even further. The Irish and Old English Catholics took to arms and slaughtered Protestant settlers in Ulster in 1641, and then formed a Catholic Confederation at Kilkenny. They supported Charles I in his struggle with the English Parliament, a clash that brought civil war, the king's execution by hanging and the establishment of the Commonwealth by Oliver Cromwell.

In 1649, Cromwell and his army rampaged through Ireland, exacting revenge on a people he considered primitive, savage and superstitious both for their support of the monarchy and for the uprising against the Protestant settlers eight years before. Ireland was now considered conquered territory, and by the time Cromwell returned to London the following year, more than a quarter of the entire island's land had been confiscated.

Under the Act of Settlement (1652), the expropriated land was parcelled out to Cromwell's soldiers and supporters. The majority of Catholic landowners in Ulster, Leinster and Munster were dispossessed and exiled to the harsh, infertile lands of Connacht.

The percentage of land in native Irish hands fell from 59 per cent in 1641 to 22 per cent in 1688. Ireland had become a land of great estates owned by outsiders.

Equally catastrophic for Gaelic Ireland was the defeat of James II, a Catholic convert whom the Irish had supported over the Protestant William III at the Battle of the Boyne in Leinster in 1690. William's victory saw Irish landownership fall to less than 10 per cent by the turn of the eighteenth century and led to the promulgation of the draconian Penal Laws (or 'Popery Code' as it was then known). These laws laid down fines and imprisonment for anyone participating in Catholic (and, in Ulster, Presbyterian) worship and severe penalties, including death, for priests who practised their ministry. Other laws barred Catholics from owning land, voting, holding public office and, importantly for the language, setting up schools and teaching.

The dispossession of the Irish and the Anglo-Irish nobility left the bards, the protectors of the Irish language, without patrons; clearly the English-speaking newcomers would have no need of their services. The task fell to independent poets such as Dáibhidh Ó Bruadair and Aodhagán Ó Rathaille who, though they were banned from printing their satirical and often defiant verse, could write it out in longhand and circulate it to those Irish speakers who could read it. By the end of the seventeenth century, however, those numbers were falling drastically. Irish poetry from this period speaks of the end of an era, as if the bards and poets sensed that they were the last of a dying breed.

Irish remained dominant in Ireland but was under extreme pressure from English; the downward spiral that had begun with the Great Plantation of Ulster would eventually bring Irish to the brink of death. Ó Bruadair satirised 'the lip-dry and simpering English tongue' while Ó Rathaille wrote the first of the *aisling* (vision) poems in which a maiden, representing Ireland, would appear, distressed and sorrowful but ever hopeful that she would one day return to her former glory.

The position of the Irish language continued to languish and by the end of the eighteenth century Irish was confined almost exclusively to the rural poor living in the west, north-west and south-west of the island; English had become the language of the powerful. The laws denying civil rights to both Catholics and Presbyterians under what had now become known as the Protestant Ascendancy in Ireland did untold damage to Irish literacy. The underground system of 'hedge schools', in which lessons were taught clandestinely, made education available to some, however. Emigration, which would become a mainstay of economic survival for many Irish people over the next two centuries, began with large numbers of Scotch Irish leaving Ulster for North America at the end of the eighteenth century. It would only get worse.

Some English argued that the only way to win Irish Catholics over to the Protestant faith was by publishing books and preaching in the vernacular. And there would be an added advantage. John Richardson wrote in *A Proposal for the Conversion of the Popish Natives* in 1712, for example, that it was 'the only way to convert such of the natives, as do not understand English', adding 'their interest will soon induce them to speak English'. The idea met great resistance from the established Anglican Church of Ireland.

The Catholic Church in Ireland did little in the way of supporting or encouraging the use of Irish. It published virtually nothing in the language and accepted English as the language of instruction at its seminary college in Maynooth, which had been founded by the government in 1795, two years after most, though not all, of the Penal Laws had been abolished. Undoubtedly this had a profoundly negative effect on the attitude of Irish speakers towards their own language at a time when Gaelic pride was reaching its nadir.

Catechisms and other religious tracts were the only Irish-language books in print in the eighteenth century. A few poets such as Brian Mac Giolla Meidhre (Brian Merriman), whose satirical *Cúirt an Mheán Oíche* (*The Midnight Court*) touched upon issues as current as celibacy among priests and feminism, and the blind bard Antoine Ó Reachtabhra, known to history as Raifteirí, were active in Clare and Mayo, but most others had gone underground and were in effect writing for themselves: by this time most of the Irish-speaking population was illiterate.

The century did not close without one final defeat and subsequent punishment. In 1798 a rebellion by the Society of United Irishmen, a radical association inspired by the revolutions in France and America and counting both Presbyterians and Catholics among its membership, broke out, with the fighting particularly heavy in Ulster and Wexford. The revolt, which is still remembered in verse and folksongs such as *The Rising of the Moon*, was put down and its leader, Theobald Wolfe Tone, committed suicide by cutting his own throat while awaiting execution. The uprising brought about the Act of Union (1800), which saw the separate Irish Parliament merged with the British one in London, and Ireland and Great Britain joined to form the United Kingdom. Ireland could no longer claim even the most remote vestiges of independence.

Despite the vicissitudes visited upon Irish over more than a millennium, the great defeats and the minor victories from the time of the first Viking raids to the Act of Union, the nineteenth century would prove to be the most critical in the language's 2500-year history. Disappearing at an accelerated rate during the first half of the century, Irish would receive its first kiss of life at the eleventh hour through conscious efforts to save and revive it. Whether this help came too late is still being discussed in the twenty-first century, but without it the disintegration of the Irish language surely would have been complete.

It is startling to see how quickly the position of Irish as a spoken language changed in a period of just 100 years. In 1799 more than 44 per cent of an estimated population of 5.4 million spoke Irish, with almost 15 per cent speaking that language alone. A shaded map would show most areas of the island, with the exception of the north-east and the eastern counties surrounding Dublin, to be predominantly Irish-speaking. By 1851, when the first census recording the number of Irish speakers was taken, the percentage of Irish speakers had dropped to 23 per cent of the total population, then more than 6.5 million. Less than 5 per cent of them were monoglots. Most Irish speakers were clustered on the coast to the south-west and west, with a small pocket in the north-west.

The 1901 census counted a total population of just under 4.5 million, of which about 14 per cent of the people spoke Irish. By that time less than half a per cent of them – about 21,000 people – were monolingual Irish speakers. The areas with predominantly Irish-speaking populations were limited to fringe areas of a half-dozen counties and do not look unlike the individual Gaeltachts as they appear on official government maps today.

There are many reasons for this dramatic downturn. The earlier collapse of the traditional wool trade and the industrial revolution in Britain had a disastrous effect on the local economy; the rural population grew poorer and at the same time larger. The growth of the towns and cities as well as improved transport and communications exposed areas previously isolated to greater outside influences. The two most important factors for the massive reduction in the number of Irish speakers, however, were the devastation caused by the so-called Great Famine and the mass emigration that followed.

The potato was introduced to Europe from the New World around 1540. By the end of the seventeenth century it had replaced oats as Ireland's most important staple crop. Within just 100 years most of rural Ireland was entirely dependent on the tuber for its diet, and the potato was consumed in large quantities in the towns and cities as well. Ireland's population had increased exponentially to more than eight million people by 1840, putting even more pressure on the land.

In 1845, a blight struck the one or two high-yielding varieties of potato grown in Ireland, bringing a partial loss of the crop. A succession of almost complete failures from 1846 to 1849 had devastating results, particularly on the rural, Irish-speaking population. More than a million people died of starvation or related diseases such as typhus, relapsing fever and dysentery, and an estimated one and a half million others left Ireland for North America, Britain and Australia.

Emigration did not stop after the worst effects of the famine had passed by the mid-nineteenth century. Huge numbers of people, evicted from their homes by new landlords determined to collect rents that had been left outstanding during the famine, joined relatives in America or sought work in the industrialised cities and shipping ports in Britain. This pattern continued for the rest of the century and into the next. By the time the independent Irish Free State was established in 1922, the entire population was barely half of what it had been before the famine. In fact, many people still remember the buses that came to pick up emigrants from small towns and villages throughout Ireland and take them to Britain; between 50,000 and 80,000 people left Ireland each year in the 1950s and early 1960s. Ireland has still not fully recovered: there are three million fewer people on the island today than there were a century and a half ago.

As most of the emigrants were the rural poor and Irish-speaking, the language was dealt a life-threatening, if not mortal, blow in numbers and in the general attitudes towards it. Irish was now reviled as the language of 'penury, drudgery and backwardness', despised as the medium of the dispossessed. English had become the language of education, survival and advancement, both for those staying behind and those leaving for their new homes.

The national school system, established in 1831, provided elementary education in the English language to those who could afford it. Education would not become compulsory – and free – for all until the end of the century, but the effect of English language education on Irish speakers spurred the rapid shift from one language to the other.

Children were punished for speaking Irish in the classroom and, through the collusion of parents and the schools, faced the wrath of their teachers if they spoke it at home. Irish-speaking parents would tie knots in a cord hung around their children's necks or make notches on a 'tally rod' every time they uttered a word in Irish. They were anxious for their children to survive in a world where the English language seemed the only way to escape the poverty they had endured and to improve their social status. As one writer put it: 'The Irish may love their language, but they love their children more'.

With no schools available to teach children to read and write in Irish, virtually all Irish speakers in Ireland were illiterate by the middle of the nineteenth century. At the same time, writers and poets received no assistance from patrons as they had in the past – who would be able to support them and even read their works? As a result, literary activity in the Irish language came to a standstill. By the close of the century the number of Irish-language books in print totalled less than two dozen.

Though the nineteenth century was a period of great decline for the Irish language, it was also when the seeds of the Gaelic Revival were first sown. From this resurgence of interest in the Irish language and its literature as well as folklore and culture, groups emerged that would eventually see Irish made the first official language of an independent Irish state, compulsory in schools for all and an integral part of the nation's cultural fabric.

Not surprisingly, given the attitudes towards the language, the revival of Irish did not originate among native speakers in the Gaeltacht or, for that matter, even among Catholics. In the first half of the century it was largely English-speaking, middle-class Protestants who became interested in the origins of Celtic culture and the Irish language itself. These 'antiquarians', as they became known, were behind the establishment of various associations, including the Gaelic Society in 1808. Its objectives included studying and preserving the Irish language but often as an historical oddity rather than an entity that still lived and breathed, however tenuously, in various pockets of the country. A decade later another society, this time backed by the Protestant Church of Ireland, was established to promote the education of native Irish and proselytise through the medium of Irish.

Many native speakers, Irish Catholics and the Catholic Church itself appeared ambivalent on the matter of the Irish language and its revival. Daniel O'Connell, the 'Liberator' instrumental in getting the Emancipation Act (1829) passed that removed the last of the anti-Catholic Penal Laws, and a native speaker himself, saw Irish as a hindrance to national development. 'The superior utility of the English tongue, as the medium of modern communication,' he wrote to a friend in 1833, 'is so great that I can witness without a sigh the gradual disuse of the Irish.'

In the last quarter of the nineteenth century, the campaign for Home Rule and the success of the so-called Land League in securing fair rents and the possibility of tenants owning their own land gave impetus to the nationalist movement and renewed interest in the Irish language. Ireland was not alone in this. The Irish revival movement was part of a larger European trend, particularly within the Celtic areas, in which romantic, nationalistic efforts were made to transform the 'Celtic Twilight' into the 'Celtic Renaissance'.

A number of voluntary societies with neither political nor religious affiliations initially were founded to preserve the Irish language and to use it as a focus for cultural nationalism. One of them – the Society for the Preservation of the Irish Language – even managed to secure a moderate place for the Irish language in primary schools as early as 1879. The most important and ultimately influential of all the associations, however, was Conradh na Gaeilge, the Gaelic League, founded in 1893 by Douglas Hyde, an Irish-language scholar and author who would later be elected as the first president of Ireland.

The Gaelic League sent *timirí* (messengers) around Ireland to set up branches to teach Irish. There were 600 by 1908 and enrolment skyrocketed, with some 50,000 people studying the language. It also established Irish-language summer schools and colleges in the Gaeltacht, a network that is still very much alive today, so that learners could immerse themselves in the language among native speakers. In 1897 the League sponsored the first Oireachtas, a literary and cultural festival that is held annually in Ireland even now.

The Gaelic League was not without its detractors. There were criticisms almost from the start about the League's 'direct method' of teaching, whereby only Irish was spoken to adults who had left school a long time previously and may never have even heard the language spoken before. Some of the teachers employed by the League were illiterate in Irish, and the beginning texts, called *Ceachtanna Simplidh* (*Simple Lessons*), were said to be too easy. As a result, a large percentage of enthusiastic beginners dropped out when things got increasingly more difficult. But all in all, the League was instrumental in promoting and preserving the Irish language at its most desperate hour. In doing so it opened the door to the possibility of bilingualism across the country, and it influenced state policies towards the language after independence.

Along with efforts to advance the cause of the spoken language, the League set its sights on the written word, publishing what little writing remained available in Irish and promoting the development of a modern, more relevant literature. The Gaeltacht, where *caint na ndaoine* (speech of the people or vernacular) was still spoken as a first language, would be the spawning ground for this writing.

The League faced a number of problems in trying to develop a new literature in Irish. With so little available in written form there was a desperate need for standardisation of the language, but this would only come gradually over the next half-century, with state support in producing grammars, dictionaries and textbooks. And there was great variation in the dialects of Irish, which had emerged as early as the seventeenth century due to isolation, bad communications and the abrupt end of most literary activity. The differences heard not just in Munster, Connacht and Ulster but within separate areas of those three provinces were divisive, and a standard would have to be established. The dialect of Munster, an area of great literary activity in the past, was first mooted as the model for a standardised language but this was, understandably, resisted by speakers in Connacht and Ulster.

Among the earliest writings in the new Irish literature were short stories, notably those by Patrick Pearse, the nationalist leader executed for his role in the aborted Easter Rising, and Pádraic Ó Conaire. Under his pseudonym, An Craoibhín Aoibhinn (The Delightful Little Branch), Douglas Hyde himself wrote the first play staged in Irish. A novel called *Séadna*, based on a folktale about a man who sold his soul to the devil and written by a priest named Peadar Ó Laoghaire, was serialised in the bilingual *Irisleabhar na Gaedhilge* (*Gaelic Journal*) from 1894 to 1901.

The Gaelic League became increasingly political and militant in the second decade of the twentieth century and by 1915 had committed itself to armed struggle to gain Ireland's independence from Britain. As a result of this, Hyde resigned as League president. When the Irish Free State, the independent twenty-six counties that make up the Republic of Ireland today, was approved in 1922, it was not surprising that the new government turned to the League for its own language principles and policies.

The Irish language became an integral part of the school curriculum at the primary and secondary levels and a pass in the subject was made a requirement for the School Leaving Certificate, roughly the equivalent of British A levels or an American high school diploma, throughout the country. Civil servants, teachers and the police all had to demonstrate a certain level of Irish in order to obtain positions. Government policy also dictated that Irish and English had equal status in public notices and official documents.

The reported numbers of Irish speakers grew substantially, inflated by pupils and students who claimed the ability to speak the language but usually abandoned it at the conclusion of their studies. However, from the birth of the Free State to the ratification of the *Bunreacht na hÉireann* (Constitution of Ireland) in 1937 that proclaimed the independent state of Éire, the population of native speakers fell by half to about 100,000 in the Gaeltacht. The constitution enshrined Irish as 'the first official language' (*an phríomhtheanga oifigiúil*) with English the second or, more accurately, 'the other official language' (*an teanga oifigiúil eile*). As to which language would take precedence in the event of dispute, the constitution was clear: 'The text in the national language shall prevail'. In the Irish version 'the national language' is expressed as *Gaeilge*.

The new state actively promoted writing in Irish, especially through a publishing unit called An Gúm (The Scheme) established in 1926, and this was one of its greatest successes. By the 1940s a whole body of new work was available in the language.

The most popular genres in the Irish language in the first half of the twentieth century were autobiographies and reminiscences written by people living in the Gaeltacht, especially on the Great Blasket, the largest of a group of islands off the coast of Kerry and now abandoned. Among the best known – selections of which are still widely read in Irish-language classes at home and abroad – are the works by the master storyteller Peig Sayers, *Fiche Bliain ag Fás* (*Twenty Years A-Growing*) by Muiris Ó Súileabháin (Maurice O'Sullivan) and, perhaps the best example of the genre and one that has certainly stood the test of time, *An tOileánach* (*The Islandman*) by Tomás Ó Criomhthain (Tomás O'Crohan). It is a rich and priceless portrait of a people and a society that have now disappeared.

The publication of these 'simple' stories and recollections sparked several parodies, including *An Béal Bocht* (*The Poor Mouth*) by Flann O'Brien, written under yet another one of his pen names (in this case Myles na gCopaleen). Some people found them brilliant satires of books that seemed to promulgate the notion of Irish being related to poverty, back-breaking work and uniqueness. Others thought them caustic, even scurrilous, reactions by writers who had bowed too deeply before the colonisers.

One thing is clear, the Gaeltacht books dealt a death blow to the folklore man – the one fighting the storms and eking out a living on a wind-swept island – as custodian of the Irish language and introduced modern characters with modern problems: urban alienation, unemployment and emigration. Máirtín Ó Cadhain wrote short stories and an outstanding novel called *Cré na Cille* (*Churchyard Dust*), published in 1953. Among the most celebrated poets were Seán Ó Ríordáin, Máire Mhac an tSaoi and Máirtín Ó Direáin. Even writers better known for their work in English contributed to the Irish opus. Liam O'Flaherty, a native speaker born on Inishmore, wrote some twenty short stories in Irish, and two plays by Brendan Behan, *The Quare Fellow* (1956) and *The Hostage* (1958), were written in Irish first and then translated into English.

Despite all these efforts and advances, the motivation and high-mindedness in learning Irish in the days when the Gaelic League was a voluntary and non-partisan body began to dissipate once language had become part of state policy. As one historian put it: 'It gave people a stick with which to beat the language.'

Irish was no longer seen as a weapon in the fight for autonomy and independence – that had already been achieved. International pressure was great and monoglot English speakers considered themselves just as Irish as their Irish cousins in the Gaeltacht, seeing no reason to learn a language that was still considered the tongue of the dispossessed or, at the very least, country bumpkins.

Éamon de Valera, the dominant figure of Irish politics in the twentieth century who served three terms as Taoiseach (prime minister) and fourteen years (1959–1973) as president, had a different vision. It was of a rural-based Ireland where Irish would be spoken universally within just a few years if it were taught to the young at an early age. That would have required nothing short of a miracle – the numbers of native speakers had dropped far too low for Irish to become the nation's official language in reality as well as on paper – but the machinery was in place. As de Valera tellingly put it: 'Ireland with its language and without freedom is preferable to Ireland with freedom and without its language.'

The candy had been taken away from the baby and its squeals

ignored throughout much of the nineteenth century. Now the child was being offered sweets and the brat was spitting them out. It was going to have to be taught how to like the candy or be force-fed it. This force-feeding of the language inspired a resistance that would continue throughout most of the twentieth century.

Infants' classes were conducted entirely in Irish and most subjects at the national schools outside the Gaeltacht were taught in that language. But the complexity of the Irish language and the great differences from English daunted even enthusiastic students. The language was taught in an old-fashioned, grammatical way, and there was the problem of textbooks, with many teachers using hastily translated versions of existing English-language ones.

Few students outside the Gaeltacht got the chance to practise at home or in their neighbourhoods and, aside from *cúpla focal*, the requisite 'few words', forgot most of the language after they'd left school. 'Instruction through the medium' of Irish was now dubbed 'instruction through the tedium' and was resisted. Detractors argued that learning such demanding disciplines as mathematics and science through Irish was retarding intellectual growth. As early as the 1940s, most schools outside the Gaeltacht had reverted to English as the language of instruction for all subjects but Irish.

There were some attempts to make the language itself more accessible. Irish underwent a series of linguistic reforms between 1945 and 1958 that simplified spelling and, to a degree, grammar; words like *saoghal* (life) and *ceartachadh* (correction) became *saol* and *ceartú*. Methods of instruction improved. There was a move away from reading, analysis of classic texts and translations, and Irish was being taught to the young in a more lively and communicative way through songs, skits and poems. This influenced the attitudes of children towards the language a great deal. At secondary level, however, as the demands of other coursework and exams mounted, Irish was still considered a drudge – almost torture – with little use, and the least favourite subject for the majority of students. 'Irish is our language of humiliation and pain,' the playwright Frank McGuinness once said, and the majority of his compatriots would probably have agreed with him.

Although it remains a required subject for all pupils and students at state-supported schools, a mandatory pass in Irish in order to obtain the School Leaving Certificate was dropped in 1973. Students who take the exam in Irish, however, get a 10 per cent marking advantage so most do. The exam remains a prerequisite for entering the national university and its associated colleges.

Successive governments continued to support the Irish language to a greater or lesser degree, especially in the Gaeltacht. The borders of the Irish-speaking districts, established in 1926, were drastically modified under the Gaeltacht Act of 1956. Children studying through the medium of Irish there were provided with a *deontas* (grant) to encourage them to continue to do so. Raidió na Gaeltachta (Gaeltacht Radio) began broadcasting in 1972 after much agitation by Irish speakers of the so-called Gaeltacht Civil Rights Movement, which had formed a pirate station. Údarás na Gaeltachta (Gaeltacht Authority), a semi-autonomous body, was established in 1979 to promote the economy of the Irish-speaking areas and thereby help preserve the language.

Outside the Gaeltacht, Irish continued to play a relatively insignificant role in economic and cultural life; most of the places reserved for the language were ceremonial or trivial. The language was extolled as the nation's 'crowning cultural asset', the 'key to national identity and distinctiveness' and a 'totem of nationhood'.

Most people favoured the government's support and assistance; no-one wanted to see the language die out altogether. Bilingual traffic and street signs were fine, and protocol demanded that politicians spout off a couple of words or a sentence in Irish at official functions. It was a symbol of Irishness, one 'connected with recollections that twine around the hearts of Irishmen', in the words of Daniel O'Connell. A majority of people, some 65 per cent in fact, agreed in a 1997 Bord na Gaeilge survey that the language was a vital part of the national culture, and 80 per cent were in favour of bilingual signs.

Having Irish enshrined in the constitution as the nation's official language was considered hypocritical by many people. Early efforts to make everyone learn the language properly had clearly failed, they said, and the government should drop the pretence of Irish being the first language. The aim of the ruling Fianna Fáil party, founded by de Valera in 1926, 'to restore and promote the Irish language as the living language of the people' was viewed as lip service, a platform based in history and retained for political expediency. Apart from a few die-hard language activists, no-one thought for a moment that Ireland would or could ever become universally bilingual. If you gave your name in Irish outside the Gaeltacht it was assumed that you were a nationalist, an activist or a teacher of the language.

The government's two-faced attitude towards the language was illustrated all too well by its failure to have Irish made an official working language of the Common Market when it joined that body in 1973, citing the burden of interpretation and translation. It remains just a treaty language of the Common Market's successor, the European Union, and is the only official language of a member state not to have equal status with those of other member states.

In the 1990s there was a general shift in attitude towards Irish among much of the population, especially those living outside the Gaeltacht. Native speakers no longer felt hesitant or embarrassed at using the language in public; secondary learners ceased looking upon it as the domain of nationalists and earnest activists at best and the language of yokels with no future at worst. Irish had hardly experienced a renaissance; it was more a modest recovery after Irish-language schools in areas that have never had them before, a popular entertainment medium and a higher self-regard in being Irish had all helped to lower resistance to it. In relation to what had happened to the language since independence, however, it was a fundamental change – one that even a group of foreign students of the language would feel somewhere in the back of beyond in Connemara.

Chapter VI

Aspirated and Eclipsed

I needn't have concerned myself, not even for a moment, about the size of the intermediate class when we first took our places in the *halla*, a large classroom in the centre's newer building that smelled slightly of damp and gave on to a large back garden.

From the start, all of my classmates were as enthusiastic as Gaelic League students opening their *Ceachtanna Simplidh* texts for the first time. The reasons for this group's eagerness – so far removed from that dynamic era of hope and change a century before – continued to mystify me but, then again, so did mine. Everyone was on a quest of their own, and the Gaelic was the grail.

The thought did enter my mind that the considerations might be less quixotic. The relatively high tuition fees could have been spurring a few people on; they might just have been trying to get their money's worth. It was unlikely, though, judging from how wide-eyed and keen almost everyone looked so early every morning.

Any doubts I'd had about our teacher's ability to bring us into the fold and have us soon bleating *as Gaeilge* were dispersed as quickly as my concerns about class size. She was an attractive and dynamic fifty-something from Baile an Fheirtéaraigh (Ballyferriter) in County Kerry and, with her cheeky grin and bright eyes, she might have been an actress dispatched by Central Casting to play 'the Irish character'.

Nuala grabbed hold of the class' enthusiasm from the first day and didn't let go for the length of the course, working us like a drill sergeant from morning to late afternoon on weekdays and for half a day on Saturday. She'd coax, she'd cajole, she'd repeat her questions over and over to get the exact response she was seeking, which she inevitably did. She was encouraging, too. After a couple of days I expressed my reservations about the level of the class and my ability to keep up. She told me I was doing fine and advised me to remain in the *meánrang* and take away from it as much as I could. And that's just what I did.

Nuala had a quirky sense of humour and shared with so many of her compatriots at home and abroad a trait as Irish as the gift of the gab: she loved to tease. She gave as much as she got from the class clown, a New Yorker in his thirties called Brian. And she'd rib me gently about smoking behind the language centre in the morning, almost suggesting I was doing something illicit amid all the signs banning ball playing and running dogs. I knew for a fact that she herself sat in the back seat of her parked car, puffing away and shifting papers before class began; I'd seen her doing it several times as I rode by on my bicycle. But I never acknowledged that and certainly never challenged her. I was the student and she was the teacher. I liked being in that relationship again.

The days were fairly regimented, each hour apportioned, and we all settled into the routine effortlessly. I found it a pleasant form of torture to be sitting on the edge of my chair in the morning, anxiously waiting to be asked what I had for breakfast, whether I'd attended the previous evening's lecture or trying to avoid dispensing any incriminating details of what mischief we'd all been up to the night before at An Chistin, a pub called 'The Kitchen' in the centre of An Cheathrú Rua.

We were fifteen in the intermediate class, just over half of us Americans of Irish extraction (to a greater or lesser degree). The rest were a mixture of Swiss, German, Catalan, Canadian, Welsh and Irish from the north and the south. As is common in situations where people share a common goal and are in one another's company throughout most of the day and evening, before long almost everyone in the class had assumed – or been conferred – a role of some sort. There was Morgan, an affable student from Boston

College and an organiser; her dreamy classmate and my best friend, Kate; the comedian Brian; and Yvonne from Belfast, who had dropped her real first name, Nuala, for reasons of political expediency in her youth and whose maternal instincts made her surrogate mother to us all. We nicknamed Jeremy, the Welsh-speaking vicar who also knew Breton, 'Super Celt' and there was the all-knowing academic from Berkeley we called Tómas Mór (Big Thomas) to distinguish him from Tómasín (Little Thomas) in the advanced class.

Despite the regimentation and hard work, there was no short-age of antics and jokes, preferably *as Gaeilge* in our teacher's presence. Sometimes we'd trade places, ostensibly for a change of scenery but really to tease and confound Nuala. She never rose to the bait, though, firing away her questions and hitting the right target every time.

The look and sound of Irish baffled me at first, but I was doing my best to take it on board, even learning some pronunciation from the way Irish place names were rendered in English. After all, Baile na hAbhann didn't sound unlike Ballynahown to untrained ears and Uachtar Ard was fairly close to Oughterard. If I lengthened the vowels a bit and trilled the 'Rs' when asking how to get to Leitir Móir, I'd reach Lettermore in no time. My method wasn't foolproof but it was fun, and it would certainly take me where I wanted to go.

One day during a tea break – this being rural Ireland, the work-day was awash with them – I remarked to a classmate that many people around us seemed to be picking up Irish with relative ease, scaling the hurdles of grammar and pronunciation with remarkably few grunts and groans along the way. Sean, a font of linguistic and most other forms of knowledge, who had a way of explaining almost everything intellectually – from the weather to the pulling of a pint of Guinness – talked about Jung's theory of collective uncon-scious and racial memory. The concept supposed that people had a storehouse of feelings and ideas inherited from their ancestral past, the innate ability to retain aspects of a previous culture, including the knowledge of a long-abandoned language, even though they'd been separated from it for generations. I told him I liked the idea of getting a genetic head start with Irish but wished racial memory would kick in a bit quicker if it really did exist. I still couldn't seem to get my tongue around all those vowels.

A poster in An Chistin showed the Olympic gold medallist Michelle Smith proclaiming: '*Is teanga álainn í an Ghaeilge* (Irish is a beautiful language)'. I wasn't sure I agreed with Michelle but didn't think I should express that opinion too publicly; the pub's owners, a pride of Irish-speaking brothers each bigger and butcher than the next, might not take kindly to that notion.

Irish was rich in idiom, of great historical interest and challenging, yes. But was it beautiful? When I heard them speak Irish, Connemara people sounded like they were swallowing dry breadcrumbs, and all the gutturals, fricatives and plosives the language called its own would have brought Irish more than a just a few demerits at any linguistic beauty contest.

After Aunt Alice had made herself more comfortable and had resigned herself to the fact that there weren't forty words for green in Irish but just two – *glas* for anything found in nature and *uaine* for man-made green things – I asked her what the Gaelic sounded like to her. 'Jewish,' she said, without hesitation. 'Just like Jewish with all those harsh sounds.'

'What do you mean by Jewish?' I asked her. 'Hebrew? Yiddish?' I wasn't trying to be a wise guy but she must have thought I was. She might have had a point, though. Both of those languages sounded rather guttural, come to think of it.

'Oh, you're full of moxie, you are. Always have been,' she said. 'You know what I'm talking about. Jewish. We heard a group of them talking on the bus when we were going to visit May. They were eating sandwiches and drinking soup from a thermos bottle. And talking. It sounded like they were clearing their throats. It was awful, that bus. I fell off the toilet when it went around a corner, remember?' She began to laugh.

I did remember that, and almost everything else connected with the trip – only God knows how or why. The heady smell of gasoline when we boarded the bus at the Greyhound station, the diner where we stopped for a break, the unfamiliar accents of the radio DJs as we drove through New York City and through the sprawl of northern New Jersey, the visit to the Brandywine River Museum in Chadds Ford, Pennsylvania, where you could watch film clips by pushing a button that was heat-sensitive. Space-age stuff it was for then. I recalled the trip as I did the tunes to all those television sitcoms and advertising jingles that I could sing from beginning to end, no matter how many verses there were. That was more like spatial than racial memory and about as useful as a Zippo lighter in hell.

Just the two of us had taken a trip to visit my Aunt May in Delaware. I was as excited as any twelve-year-old kid would be escaping from parents, sisters and brothers, home. May was Alice's sister and married to a Protestant of German extraction. That was different, that was good and I wanted to know more. But I got into trouble when he asked me to repeat the *Confiteor Dei*, the long Latin prayer altar boys had to memorise and mumble in order to serve at Mass. 'You wouldn't be interested,' I told him.

I was trying to provoke some response; I wanted to know what he thought of Catholics and the saints and May going to Mass every Sunday alone. But Uncle John's Protestantism was something we weren't ever supposed to acknowledge (much less mention), like sex and suicide. Alice was furious, as angry as she'd got when I stepped on her toes the day before. She had corns and bunions and all those other things women got from wearing high heels too small for them. That's what my mother said. And I was always stepping on her feet. 'Watch that tongue of yours, Mr Smarty Pants,' she said sternly, 'or I'll wash it out for you.'

I smiled to myself as I remembered her words. 'That's just what I told you,' Alice said in acknowledgement. 'Call me old-fashioned but I'll say it again if you get out of hand in English or the Gaelic.'

She'd left herself wide open for me to do just that: 'Al, you're old-fashioned!' But we'd done that joke to death all those years back on the front porch looking out onto Sedalia Road and she didn't laugh. 'But do you think it sounds familiar at all, the Gaelic?' I asked her. 'You must have heard Sean telling me about racial memory the other day. I'm sure you did. You're always eavesdropping on me.'

'That's a load of old movie,' she said, using her word for doo-doo, for shit. I hadn't heard that one for a very long time. I couldn't tell whether she was commenting on the idea of remembering things from the ancestral past or denying that she listened in on every one of my conversations (which she most definitely did), but didn't get a chance to ask her. 'None of it is like the way we used to say the words,' she said. 'The Gaelic just sounds foreign to me.'

I wasn't expecting to feel anything in particular once I'd managed to read a simple paragraph or understand what a newspaper headline or an advertisement was trying to tell or sell me in Irish. Reading is a passive activity and understanding comes to anyone if they stare at a phrase or sentence long enough. The odd thing was that with racial memory lurking – possibly – in my subconscious, I thought it would be different writing in the language for the first time. I figured that since my grandparents didn't have any Irish and everyone before them had been illiterate, it wouldn't be just me writing for the first time but the whole clan. I didn't anticipate tongues of fire or a white bird hovering above my head; I would have settled for just a shiver of recognition. Yet I felt nothing beyond the usual concerns of misspelling a word or mixing the present with the past tense. Learning Irish was just like studying any other new language: confusing, challenging and, as Alice had put it, foreign.

All foreign languages are difficult to learn well, no matter how familiar or easy they may seem at the beginning, and Irish is no exception. It is a highly inflected language, particularly in verb conjugations, and it can be very hard coming to grips with the way the verb changes, bearing less and less resemblance to its root as it trips through the tenses. *Téann mé* is 'I go', *chuaigh mé* 'I went' and *rachaidh mé* 'I will go'. You also need to know *An ndeachaigh mé?*, 'did I go?', and *Ní dheachaigh mé,* 'I didn't go'.

And those are just the verbs; nouns and adjectives go through some pretty bizarre mutations too. All nouns in Irish have masculine or feminine gender and are declined – they take special endings – to show their function in the sentence, be it genitive (possessive) or dative (indirect object). Simply addressing someone requires the use of a special case called the vocative. If I were to call for Seán's attention or greet him in a letter, I'd say '*A Sheáin*', which sounds something like 'aw hyoyn'.

All languages have their own peculiarities. Hungarian builds words and phrases not from the front with prefixes and prepositions but with affixes and postpositionals stuck on the back. Slovene not only counts one thing (singular number) and numerous things (plural number) but two things (dual number). Some Asian languages, Chinese and Indonesian among them, don't have any verbal tenses as such, but signify the present, past and future with adverbs like 'now', 'then' and 'tomorrow'. Irish too has its own unique ways of doing things.

Among the strangest transformations that Irish undergoes is something called lenition (or aspiration). That means that nouns like *cóta* (coat) or *páiste* (child) make fundamental changes when preceded by certain words. Put *mo* (my) in front of either and they become *mo chóta* and *mo pháiste*; they look and are pronounced differently. Feminine nouns aspirate even when the definite article *an* (the) comes before them: *fuinneog* is 'window' or 'a window' while *an fhuinneog* is 'the window'; *bróg* is 'shoe' or 'a shoe' but *an bhróg* is 'the shoe'.

On the other hand, if you want to attach *ár* (our) to 'coat', 'child', 'window' or 'shoe' a complicated system called eclipsis kicks in, and you end up with phrases looking like these: *ár gcóta, ár bpáiste, ár bhfuinneog, ár mbróg*. And these rules apply even to proper nouns. When 'Boston', 'Galway' or 'Cork' are preceded by the preposition *i* (in) they metamorphose into the outlandish *i mBoston, i nGaillimh* and *i gCorcaigh*. It may be that lower-case letters supporting upper-case ones – Bank na hÉireann (Bank of

Ireland), Tír na nÓg (Land of Youth), An tSionainn (River Shannon), Béal na mBuillí (Strokestown) – eventually begin to look normal, but I suspect it's something you have to be born with. I still feel the urge to make all those little letters big ones.

It's probably not fair to say, given the anomalies of the English language, but I've always been suspicious of languages that do not have words for 'yes' and 'no', something that Irish shares with Chinese. To repeat the verb in order to affirm or to negate seems to me a convoluted and uneconomical way of answering a question – not to mention how primitive it sounds when you translate it into English. '*An bhfuil tú reidh?* (Are you ready?)' '*Tá* (Am)'. '*Ar bhuail tú do chara aréir?* (Did you meet your friend last night?)' '*Bhuail mé* (I met)'.

Irish has something else in common with Chinese: it sometimes uses what are called measure words. We have them to a certain extent in English; you ask for a 'piece' of paper or cheese and not 'a paper' or 'a cheese'. In Irish they are used more extensively. You cannot say 'my money' in Irish as such; it must be expressed as 'my share' or 'my part of money' (*mo chuid airgid*). Ditto for 'my hair' or even 'my Irish'. They're *mo chuid gruaige* and *mo chuid Gaeilge*.

The idiosyncrasies of this ancient tongue don't stop there. With very few exceptions, sentences begin with a verb in Irish. Native speakers will tell you they prefer it that way because they can see what's coming immediately. Think of it as a fast track to the heart of the story, something very dear to most Irish people. 'I saw the cat (*Chonaic mé an cat*)' starts with 'saw'. 'Did you drink your tea (*D'ól tú do tae?*)' begins with 'drank'.

There is no real infinitive in Irish: 'to give a speech', for example, is rendered as 'giving a speech' (*óráid a thabhairt*), 'to go to sleep' becomes 'going to sleep' (*dul a chodladh*). And there are not one but two forms of the verb 'to be', as in Spanish, for example, but learning when and how to use them in Irish is much more complex. *Tá* is used for descriptions or for things that are temporary: *tá seomra mór* (the room is big), *tá siad anseo* (they are here), *tá an lá go maith* (it's a nice day). The copula, or linking verb, *is*, on the other hand, identifies and classifies or qualifies things: *is mise Stiofán* (I am Stephen), *is bean mhaith í* (she is a good woman), *is dochtúir é Tomás* (Thomas is a doctor).

Both the complexity of the Irish language and the degree to which it varies from English have daunted even the most enthusiastic students over the decades. At the same time, the tedious, grammatical way in which it was taught in schools and the dearth of real places in which to practise it outside the far-flung Gaeltacht turned many against the language. None of us at the Áras Uí Chadhain felt that way, for reasons that were both obvious and not so apparent.

We had elected to study Irish ourselves; it was not being forced upon us as some sort of requirement for entry into university or gainful employment. We were living and learning in the heart of the largest Irish-speaking district in the country. Most importantly (and gratefully), we were being taught Irish in a modern, upbeat way that would have us ordering meals in restaurants, writing emails, even telling lies in no time at all.

We weren't just learning *Gaeilge na leabhar* (book Irish) but the Irish of the home and the Gaeltacht. Along with memorising the noun declensions, the verb conjugations and why *liom* was 'with me' but *leat* 'with you', we conversed and play-acted and sang in a language that might have been foreign but was certainly coming alive. Slowly it began to make sense – sort of – but there was always a beast lying in wait and ready to nip at the heels (or worse) of anyone trying to move a bit too fast.

Those interested in reclaiming their original Irish name as their own – I would be Stiofán Ó Fallamhain, for example – were in for a challenge of no mean scale. It was fairly easy for the men. *Ó* means 'grandson' so Seán Ó Briain (John O'Brien) is the male descendant of some Brian along the way. *Mac* is 'son'; Seamus Mac Gearailt (James Fitzgerald) is the son of Gerald (or at least someone was the son of Gerald once). Since Irish has gender, *ó* just wouldn't do for Seán's sister, Mary, or Seamus' daughter,

Bridey, however. They would be called Máire Ní Bhriain and Bríd Nic Ghearailt.

As soon as anyone with an Irish name starts to own things – takes possession, so to speak – it becomes a lot more complicated. *An rothar Sheáin Uí Bhriain* is 'John O'Brien's bike' while *an teach Sheamus Mhic Ghearailt* is 'James Fitzgerald's house'. The political correctness of the New Ireland hasn't reached all aspects of the Irish language yet: 'a student' (male or female) is *mac léinn*, literally a 'son of learning', and this possessive rule applies to wives as well. If Bridey were to marry Seán, she'd become Bríd Uí Bhriain or Bean Uí Bhriain (Mrs O'Brien). Mary would be known as Máire Mhic Ghearailt (or Bean Mhic Ghearailt) should she marry Seamus.

Sometime we'd learn structures that, unlike putting verbs at the start of each sentence or repeating them to answer 'yes' or 'no', sounded familiar and felt comfortable at once. Some of the students might have thought that racial memory was beginning to perform its magic, but most recognised the patterns to be identical to the idiosyncratic and often fetching way that the Irish people speak the English language. *Fein* – 'himself' or 'herself' but meaning 'he' or 'she' as in 'I'm just after seeing himself/herself in the pub' – peppered every other sentence. Another example was the use of the verbal noun for continuous meaning. 'I am sitting' is literally 'I am in my sitting' (*tá mé i mo shuí*) in Irish while 'he is sleeping' is phrased as 'he is in his sleep' (*tá sé ina chodladh*). And when 'I am in my solitude' (*tá mé i m'aonar),* meaning 'alone', usually 'I am in my silence' (*tá mé i mo thost*).

At other times, Irish would make *too* much sense – as surprising as that may sound for such a difficult language. When we'd be practising dialogues in class or translating sentences at home, I'd be surprised how similar in structure the Irish result was to the English. I found myself wondering whether the language, having borrowed – willingly or not – so much from English over the centuries, had become a hybrid, a kind of 'neo-Irish' simplified to welcome everyone on board.

Did native Irish speakers really say *'tabhair aire'* (literally, 'take care') at the end of their letters and conversations a century ago? Would the women of the Great Blasket at the time Tomás Ó Criomhthain was writing *The Islandman* have called out '*Tóg go bóg é!* (Take it easy!)' to their menfolk as they boarded their *naomhóg* and embarked on another fishing expedition? Would a farmer leading a horse and buggy on one of the Aran Islands during the same period 'be prepared to stop' if he came across a sign reading *Bí ullamh chun stad* or would he scratch his head in bafflement at a 'Celtic Esperanto' full of neologisms and imports? Why did *an t-uafás airgid* sound exactly as we would say it in English: 'an awful lot of money'?

Irish had certainly taken much from the English language and, like *stuif* (stuff), *dusta* (dust) and *strus* (stress), it was all around us. But to be fair, it's gone the other way too; Irish has contributed a number of words to English. Many of the most obvious ones are used in reference to Irish things and situations only: shamrock, shillelagh, banshee, leprechaun, brogue, colleen and so on. Others – clan, glen, bard, druid, bog and blarney – have travelled somewhat farther afield.

Words in common usage in English that few people would suspect as having originated in Ireland run the gamut from 'whiskey' (*uisce beatha*, or 'water of life') and 'spree' (*spraoi*, for 'fun' or 'sport') to 'galore' (*go leor*, meaning 'plenty' or 'enough'). And who would have thought that *sluaghán* would give us 'slogan' and *smidiríní*, or 'little pieces', the evocative 'smithereens'? A swaggering Irish lad (*buachaill*) must have been the first 'bucko', and we're forever in debt to the Houlihan family, whose rough and lawless ways gave us 'hooligan'. Some people believe that the shout 'Fore!' when playing golf comes from the Irish *fair* for 'watch' or 'guard' and that 'smashing' as used in Britain meaning 'fine' or 'great' is a corruption of *is maith é sin* (literally, 'that's great').

When studying a foreign language, people often acquire words they hardly know or rarely use in their own tongue. *Ris de veau*

(sweetbreads) and *langoustine* (scampi) are *de rigueur* for understanding any French menu, and you won't eat many vegetables in
Hungary, where they are routinely pickled, without learning the
word *savanyú* (sour). In rural Ireland you'll need to know the word
móna (turf) if you intend to stay warm. At the same time, learners'
vocabularies can grow in a wild, somewhat disorganised fashion.
You might have the word for 'cup' but not for 'saucer', be able to
'leave' but not 'return', know 'like' but not know 'love'.

When we returned to the classroom one afternoon we noticed
the words *fuil* and *mún* written on the chalkboard. 'Yuck,' said
Jennifer, a young Swiss woman and one of the more diligent students in the intermediate class. 'That's an unappetising welcome
back to class after lunch.' The rest of us quickly ferreted through
our little green dictionaries and agreed in unison; 'blood' and
'urine' did not go down very well as post-prandial digestives.

The new vocabulary words had been provided by Josep, a
Catalan who had become interested in Irish because it too was
classified as a 'minority' or 'lesser-used' language, though one
with native speakers numbering in the tens of thousands, not mil-
lions like his. Josep was a laboratory technician who spoke
English but preferred to communicate almost entirely in Irish, not
only with local people in the pub and at the post office but with
his classmates as well. During the lunch break he'd been explaining to someone how he spent his workday analysing specimens
back in his lab in Barcelona.

As a result of introducing ourselves to Nuala and describing
what we did (or, for the younger ones in the class, were planning
to do) for a living, we learned a lot of new words. Some of them
were more useful than others. With a couple of nurses in our
midst, we took on 'check-up' and 'surgery' and the teaching pro-
fession gave us 'lecture' and 'meeting'. Almost everyone could
'play' a musical instrument (as opposed to a part on stage or a
game of cards, which demanded different kinds of 'play'). I
couldn't imagine when I would ever have to reach back into the
recesses of my memory and retrieve 'tying knots on a sailboat on
Lake Geneva' in conversation, though Jennifer would; that's how

she spent the previous summer. On the other hand, 'travel' and 'guidebook' would be in great demand among this peripatetic group. I was sure of that.

The graded stories we read in class reflected the culture of the language we were studying, as they naturally would. Take on French, and you'll soon be reading all about 'sitting at a café and watching the world go by'. Study Spanish and you'll learn more about bullfighting than you may have wanted to. Many of the Irish texts presented to us – folk tales, rags-to-riches stories, anecdotes full of black humour – did so almost to the point of cliché.

A clever horse outwits a farmer on the Great Blasket by swimming the short distance over from Beginish Island and gobbling up all the potatoes and cabbage in the man's vegetable patch. A man is concerned when the doctor treating his wife requests a knife, a hammer and a saw – until he barges into the room and sees the physician trying to open his black bag. A street sweeper who can neither read nor write rises up to become a wealthy philanthropist but remains illiterate; he would never have got rich otherwise, he said. A leprechaun toting a little hammer wreaks havoc on a classroom, spilling ink everywhere. A man assures his mate that the little people can't possibly exist. The friend happens to be a talking donkey.

The practice sentences and dialogues usually echoed Irish situations as well, and many of them were very familiar. The characters always seemed to be going to the pub, in the pub or leaving the pub (often uncharacteristically early). The sample menus we used to play-act waiters and diners in a restaurant had a choice of a dozen different meats – from *gríscínicaoireola* (mutton chops) and *bagún* (bacon) to *stobhach Gaelach* (Irish stew).

There was the penchant for high drama and just a bit of whingeing in some of the conversations. 'I worked in that supermarket myself once,' Niamh tells Liam in Lesson Twelve. 'I didn't like the work. I was but seventeen years old at the time. I was there for only five weeks.' We were all curious why Niamh disliked the job so much – dealing with the public? too few tea breaks? a lascivious boss? – but never did get to learn the reason; her bus had arrived and she was gone. And then there were the snippets of gossip embedded in the text that revealed a certain envy, a suggestion that characters might be trying to rise above their station. That was something I recognised from working-class Irish America. 'Seán and I were at the Hot Plate Restaurant on Thursday evening,' Niamh tells the same Liam. 'We saw Nóra and Úna at another table. They were drinking *wine*.'

Each day lessons followed lessons in the morning, then came lunch delivered in a large plastic cooler to the centre by the *bean an tí* herself and we returned to the classroom again for a couple more hours. At the end of the day, extracurricular activities like singing, dancing, poetry readings and lectures were punctuated by dinner, homework and regroupings in the pub for a pint or two, a game of snooker and some basic Irish conversation with whomever felt like passing the time of day with us. We felt like kids again, corralled and told what to do and when to do it, praised when we offered inspired responses or had completed our homework without mistakes, gently berated if we were out of order.

I fell asleep in class one sunny afternoon and even began to dream, the cup of water in my hand hitting the desk and spilling over my hand. *'Nach bhfuil, Stiofáin?* (Isn't that so, Steve?)' I could hear a voice asking from the front of the classroom. Nuala was none too pleased. For a moment I thought I was out at sea, drifting in the current under the warm sunshine and making no attempt to paddle toward the shore.

The lunch break and the periods before and after all the extra events were busy times for me. Although I'd been determined to leave everything in London behind me during my journey in order to concentrate fully on Irish and whatever I was seeking, it didn't work out that way. I had work obligations that needed to be addressed almost daily and whenever I found a spare moment I'd carry the laptop into the secretary's office or wherever I spied a telephone jack looking for a mate. There were proofs to read, queries to answer and captions to write for yet another guidebook that I thought I'd already bid adieu. No, crêpe does have an accent mark in French and, yes, that is the Palais de Justice in Paris but we've flopped the photo. And it was now the only way to keep in touch with Mike.

For reasons I couldn't fathom, my mobile phone could never seem to pick up a network signal at the language centre, and I seldom got to use it elsewhere. That was just as well; we were communicating at last via email. I'd considered email as just a work tool – a medium useful for speed and brevity but one where misinterpretation was a constant risk if communicating on anything beyond 'right', 'wrong', 'now' or 'later'. Yet, when Mike and I began contacting each other this way, both the immediacy and the time allowed to consider our thoughts carefully were bonuses. None of the breaking up, satellite echoes and distance tones; before us were blank screens to fill up with experiences, anecdotes, new ideas and even plans.

The phone did work when I travelled away from the school, to the end of the field behind it but I couldn't go there. Alice had warned me about it one afternoon as I headed in that direction. 'Don't walk out back,' she'd said. 'That's where the "deenee shee" live. You'll disturb them.' I didn't know what she was talking about. 'Who are they?' I asked her.

'Haven't you heard of the "deenee shee"?' she asked. 'I thought I'd told you when you were a boy. You probably weren't listening. They're the fairy people who live in the 'leesh', that mound over there. Disturb their territory and they'll spirit you away. They're nice people and the food isn't bad, but I'd be making tea from foxglove leaves till doomsday trying to get you back home. And that's where you want to be. I know that.'

I told her she was crazy, just the way I liked her. I'd never given these old superstitions any thought. In fact, until that folk tale we'd read in class, I didn't even know that the little people were supposed to be cobblers by trade. Why did they keep fitting heels and soles, hammering and stitching, when they had pots of gold at their disposal?

'Now don't get sarky. The "deenee shee" don't like you sniggering at them,' Alice told me. 'The worst crime of all is not to believe in them.' I knew I didn't and never would. How on God's green earth could I believe in *daoine sí* living in a *lios* when there I was with a mobile phone in my hand and a laptop computer under my arm? The next thing you'd know I'd be having a conversation with an ass. But I kept away from that part of the field, just in case. Foxglove tea was supposed to be good for the heart and I wasn't sure I had any need for that right now.

Chapter VII

The Wild Quarter

Our daily routine in An Cheathrú Rua offered a lot more than irregular verbs, lectures on early Irish poetry and meat and two veg (which in Ireland meant at least one type of potato). We went out in search of *siamsa*, 'entertainment' or 'fun', as often as the demands of homework, folk singing and set dancing allowed, and that was fairly regularly.

There was no need to make excuses; we were encouraged – in fact, urged – to mix and converse with local people. This was Ireland; someone would always have something to say. The problem was, once thrown out in the 'real world' of Irish, things didn't always sound the way we thought they should. I was beginning to bore myself with the punctuator *Ceart go leor* (okay) that I used when pretending to follow a conversation and the less frequent *Ní thuigim* (I don't understand) when I admitted I wasn't.

The focus of social life in An Cheathrú Rua was the pub, as it is throughout Ireland be it country town or county capital, and this settlement of perhaps 300 people could boast five. There was the An Táilliúir (The Tailor), a small, smoky little tavern near the Spar supermarket and fish and chip shop 'downtown' – if there was such a thing in An Cheathrú Rua – that attracted an older clientele. They'd glance up suspiciously when the door was opened, looking surprised and maybe even a little resentful that their space had been invaded. An Réalta was just that bit too far to entice most of us, and the aftertaste of that sour Guinness lingered, as far as I was concerned. Each of the two hotels had bars that served a mixed cocktail of Irish-speaking local people as well as well-heeled Anglophone tourists and businesspeople; the groups spoke in hushed voices among themselves and showed little interest in one another. It was clear you were supposed to behave at the hotel bars, though the atmosphere would change whenever there was a music session going on.

That left An Chistin the venue of choice for local people and outsiders. Its central location at the town crossroads made The Kitchen the most popular place in town and there was a snooker table, outside seating for when it wasn't raining and a group of affable old boys playing cards just inside the main entrance. More than once I opened the door to fetch another round for the lushes outside (I can say that for by then I was inside) only to see the cards fly off the table like a flock of startled pigeons. That's how I learned to swear in Irish.

Cursing in English, which was heard with startling regularity, was the property of passing motorists – as many of them Irish as foreign – who had lost their way trying to follow the road signs in Gaelic and were incredulous that An Clochán was the same as Clifden and Cathair na Mart – not Westport – was to be their real destination in the Connemara Gaeltacht. We spent a lot of time spreading their maps out flat on the picnic tables outside, tracing the correct route with our thumbnails and translating place names for them.

The foreign tourists were usually surprised and impressed that we were studying the 'local language', wanting us to tell them simple phrases and where they could hear it spoken. Many of the Irish motorists, especially older ones, wondered aloud why we were bothering. 'So we can tell the likes of you where to go,' I told a motorist from Dublin one sunny afternoon. I thought it was funny but he didn't. He must have been tired and annoyed at finding himself lost in his own country.

Traditional Irish music didn't seem to do much for the people of An Cheathrú Rua, judging from what was regularly on offer at the pubs. Occasionally a musician or two would find their way to the small stage in the back area of An Chistin and worry a fiddle or an amplified flute, but the music of choice was country and western. Local people were nonplussed when one of us men-

tioned that we were, well, a little disappointed. 'If you want traditional Irish music,' said one, 'you'd do better in Boston or New
York.' Country music, with its syrupy lyrics of unemployment,
leaving home, lost love and broken homes, was now as Irish as
pizza and those luridly coloured bottles of alcopop dispensed
from behind every bar. Who were we to question the musical
tastes of our hosts?

Some of my classmates played snooker, others tried to wade
through the Connemara accent in conversation with the bar staff
or card shufflers while chomping on *duileasc* (dulse, an edible
reddish-brown seaweed not unlike salty chewing gum). Everyone
drank pints of 'the black stuff' or Harp lager, though every once
in a while some comedian would trick another victim into asking
the barman for a Bud. *Bod*, pronounced very much the same way,
is the Irish word for 'penis'.

Without even realising it initially, we began to pepper our own
conversations with Irish words and phrases – I suppose it was better than restricting them to English only – in the pub or on the back
steps at the language centre during the tea breaks and lunchtime.
Then it became a self-conscious battle of wits, trying to dream up
new phrases. Something might have a certain *'níl a fhios agam'* (*je
ne sais quoi*) quality to it and *'Cén scéal?* (What's the story?)' was
the most common greeting. Someone might respond with *Diabhal
scéal*, literally, 'devil a story' meaning 'nothing at all', but almost
everyone had one in Ireland, and if they didn't they could always
make one up. We weren't going to be any different with ours –
opinionated, funny, whatever. The only difference between the
words for 'opinion' (*barúil*) and 'funny' (*barrúil*) in Irish, we
learned, was one little 'r'. Stories 'r' us indeed . . .

Even if An Chistin had a clock on its walls there was no real
need for it. The Angelus bell rang out at noon and at six each
evening, reminding anyone who had forgotten for the moment
that the New Ireland was still a Catholic country, and 'An
tAmhrán na bhFiann', the national anthem called the 'Soldier's
Song' in English, signalled closing time. This was taken very
seriously indeed – the song rather than the hurried closing of

doors and the locking of taps – and everyone stood to attention and sang along with the exception of a couple of fervent anti-nationalists who would escape through the back garden once the first chords of the peppy tune were struck.

We were all in school again and acted accordingly, sometimes more often than was prudent. Armed with a plastic bag full of takeaway cans of lager, we'd head for the high stone wall opposite the police station or as far as the beach, chatting, singing and grading the evening's stellar episodes. It all made for a lot of talk the next morning in any language.

The language centre organised a *turas* (excursion) every week or so to places like Clifden, the capital of Connemara, and Kylemore Abbey, a sprawling mock Gothic pile from the nineteenth century overlooking a pretty lake, though there wasn't an Irish speaker for miles around at either place. We also visited sites with a more obvious Gaelic connection. The first was a pilgrimage to Teach an Phiarsaigh, Patrick Pearse's cottage at An Gort Mór (Gortmore) north of An Cheathrú Rua. Pearse, a gifted writer who was executed by the British for his role in the 1916 Rising, came to the area in the early twentieth century to perfect his Irish and to write. The man who has been all but canonised by the nation produced many of his short stories and plays while living there, and the house has become a temple to Irish nationalism.

Along the way the young bus driver pointed out curiosities – a herd of Connemara ponies, the outlines of the 'lazy beds' on the hillsides where farmers once planted their potatoes – and regaled us with stories in both English and Irish. He talked about the mysterious drowning of Lady Dudley, wife of Ireland's former Lord Lieutenant, in the bay in front of Screeb Lodge almost eighty years before and about the handful of elderly Irish speakers who lived in the isolated hills to the north but still managed to walk down once a week to attend Mass. His grandfather had been a republican, he told us, and when the Black and Tans came to arrest him, he hid for three weeks under the seaweed he'd cut for twenty pence a tonne. 'It sells for sixteen pounds a tonne nowadays,' he reminded us. By the time we reached our destination, we were all ready to pay our obeisances to the saint of Irish nationalism.

The cottage was a two-room structure, whitewashed and thatched and sitting on a gentle slope some distance from the main road. We had a look at the room in which Pearse wrote many of his Irish short stories and then moved into the bedroom with its spartan furnishings and tiny windows. 'So that's where it all happened,' said Jen, looking down at the narrow bed in the centre of the room. I didn't know what had happened there and asked her what she meant.

'*Bhuel*', she began – it sounded almost like 'well' in English and that's what it meant but we liked the convoluted way it was spelled in Irish. 'There was a student on the course last year, a woman, who was in love with Pearse. Yes, of course I know he's been dead for almost a century. Didn't seem to make any difference to her though. She was infatuated with him. Knew his poems by heart and quoted lines from them. She even kept a framed picture of him on her desk and would stare at it in class for inspiration.' That sounded weird and I said so.

'The *scéal* gets even weirder, believe me,' she said. Jen always told a good story, among the best, and I leaned forward to hear it over the guide's fervent and high-speed explanation in Irish of Pearse's life and times. 'We had to write a short composition for class – I can't even remember what the subject was – but naturally the woman chose Pearse. But she didn't write anything about his politics or the Rising – all that blood sacrifice and hair shirt stuff – or even about his work. She described in great detail an affair she imagined having with him right here. In this very bed.'

I looked around the damp little room and tried to imagine the scene. What intrigued me most was how the woman in intermediate class – the very one I was attending – had managed all the vocabulary. The bed didn't look like it would accommodate one person very comfortably, never mind a couple.

I could vaguely remember a charcoal sketch I'd seen of Pearse in the National Gallery in Dublin some years before. He had fine features and what looked almost like plucked eyebrows. He wouldn't have held a candle to Michael Collins – or was I remembering the handsome 'Big Fellow' as played by Liam Neeson in the film? But he wasn't a bad-looking man. 'Didn't someone once tell me he was probably gay?' I asked Jen.

'That's what they say, but no-one knows for sure. When someone mentioned that in class though she went ballistic. Shouting and screaming. She almost started a fight. Everyone was mortified.'

'Where do you suppose she is now?' I asked Jen.

'Who knows? Probably bonking him long distance,' she said. We both looked down at the bed at the same time and grimaced. 'Perhaps we'd better leave them to it,' I said.

Once, we organised our own excursion, to Croagh Patrick, a tall mountain in southern Mayo where the 'glorious apostle' Saint Patrick is said to have spent forty days and forty nights in the distant fifth century praying and fasting *and* banishing all the snakes from Ireland. On the last Sunday in July, as an act of penance, the Catholic faithful climb to the top of what is also called the Reek. Some of the group were in a penitential mood and decided to make the pilgrimage. None would divulge why this was so, but we all had our suspicions: late nights overindulging at An Chistin and unlikely twosomes spotted abandoning the pub before the national anthem sounded – the usual sorts of guilt-inducing Catholic things. Others, 'reptiphobes' no doubt, may have been going along to thank Paddy for his serpentine expulsion trick. The rest of us jumped on for the ride and the cobweb-ridding climb more than 700 metres up, just another distraction from *téann mé*, *chuaigh mé* and *rachaidh mé*.

We could almost reach out of the bus and touch the leaden sky as we drove north through the Maumturk Mountains and past the greyish peaks of the Twelve Bens to Leenane and entered Mayo in a light rain. By the time we reached the Reek it had stopped, so that extra bit of penance had been taken away from the most zealous of the pilgrims. Still, the paths and rocks would be sufficiently slippery to make it a tougher climb than usual and the truly contrite – just how bad had they been? – were soon removing their shoes to ascend barefoot.

We embarked as a group, trudging forever upward, and chattering away with one another and those who were coming in the opposite direction. They were the ones who had risen early to watch the sunrise from the summit and were now descending looking more flushed and breathless than absolved. After a short time we began to split up into smaller groups and then break off on our own; it's climbs like these when you want to be alone, setting your own pace and breaking when you want to without a group decision having to be made. The mountain was *dubh le daoine*, 'black with people' or 'swarming' as they say in Irish, and I found myself accompanying a nun from Uganda for awhile and then an Irish-speaking family from Kerry joined me. When I tried to make conversation with them, they teased me. They didn't like the Connemara accent and said so. I passed a blind man being led by a seeing-eye dog, its paws splayed like little fans as it scrambled over the rocks.

Some of us thought the saddle of the mountain was the destination – it had looked like that from the ground with the masses of people gathering there – but when we reached it we saw that the refreshment stands had detained them. The most difficult stage of the climb was still awaiting us. A steep scree, with rocks ranging in size from oranges to basketballs, spilled down from the top in the shape of a truncated cone. People were fortifying themselves with potato chips and bottles of fizzy orange soda. I certainly wasn't fasting but I wouldn't have any of it. Not that early in the morning.

I soon discovered that the easiest way to ascend the unsteady pile of rocks and stones was to make like a crab and walk sideways or to tack like a sailboat from side to side. This was the most sensible – and safest – course, but it was a dizzying exercise. After zigzagging to and fro for awhile, I'd find myself straightening up and trying to walk forward, slipping on the rocks and feeling exposed, as if some great hand were reaching out to pluck me from behind. Earlier I'd refused the offer of a walking stick from a pilgrim coming down the path and she told me that I'd soon be regretting my decision. She was right. By the time I scrambled over the last few boulders, my torso was parallel to the ground and I was almost on my knees.

On the summit people were milling around, picnicking or listening to a continuous Mass being said by relays of priests alternating in English and Irish. The sky had cleared, and when I located some of the others in our group we all inched toward the north edge to look down on the archipelago in Clew Bay, scores of uninhabited islets and sandbanks that looked like shards of a broken china plate. In the distance was Achill Island, another Gaeltacht on its last legs.

'I didn't know those islands even existed,' said Marsha, as she began unpacking her generous contribution to our communal meal. She'd brought heaps of food and a knapsack full of 'just-in-case' items. She packed like me, carrying everything she thought she might need, but had probably made a lot of friends as a result. 'When we climbed the Reek last year, you couldn't see your foot in front of you from all the fog. The paths were a lot muddier and more slippery too.'

'So you should count on receiving a lot less sanctifying grace this time around then,' I teased her.

'At least I wasn't flown up here on a helicopter like the bishop was,' she said. 'Some pastor of the flock he is!'

Beth, one of the stragglers, arrived out of breath. 'Oh guys, what a climb! I'm exhausted!'

'But I thought climbing the Reek would be child's play for a Coloradan,' I said. 'Isn't this the sort of ant hill you all scale every morning *before* breakfast?'

Beth smirked and rolled her eyes. 'Not every morning, Steve. Just on the weekdays. We save Pikes Peak and the oxygen tanks for the weekend. No, really, I don't think I've done a climb this difficult since I was in school.' She wrinkled her nose and sniffed. 'Is that me? Now I know why they call this the Reek. But everyone was *so* helpful. I slipped and fell two or three times and someone came to my rescue and then another person offered to take my pack.'

'And I suppose a woman called Veronica offered to wipe your face with her veil,' someone shouted. 'What is this? The road to Calvary?'

We might have been joking but some of our group were taking the climb a lot more seriously than I had anticipated. Kathleen rushed over from where a group of people had formed a queue and sat down among us. 'I've just made my first confession,' she announced, her eyes so wide open they looked dilated. We looked at one another quizzically. Kathleen was a television scriptwriter from Los Angeles who wore designer clothes and drove a rental car around An Cheathrú Rua when everyone else (except me) walked. The younger people at the language centre seemed to be familiar with all the shows she'd worked on and even some of the episodes she'd written; Kathleen was something of a celebrity among them. She didn't seem the type to be making her first or her last confession on the summit of Croagh Patrick, though. I'd been surprised to see her on the bus at all that morning. Apparently she was embracing the faith.

Still she remained in true form, telling us excitedly how long the confession had taken since she'd had to recite a lifetime's worth of sins and how severe the penance was that the priest had doled out. 'Maybe you should descend the mountain barefoot like these true believers here,' I said pointing to Chris, a student from the beginners' class, and Tómasín. They were comparing the condition of their feet and counting the blisters. We'd all decided that Chris had earned more grace or plenary indulgence or whatever they were doing it for as one of his blisters was bleeding. Kathleen looked at me in mock horror. 'Are you crazy? Go barefoot?' she shrieked. 'I haven't had a pedicure in three weeks!'

When we'd finished our lunch, the weather had begun to turn again. Someone suggested making the descent immediately in order to escape the rain and to catch the coach back to An Cheathrú Rua at the appointed time. Going down was like a sport, and we scampered down the face of the scree like mountain goats, moving aside only to allow members of the rescue squad carrying an injured climber on a stretcher to pass us.

'Slow down will you, for goodness sake?' someone called from behind. 'You're going so fast and I can't keep up with you.' I turned around. It was Alice, still in heels but leaning on the very staff I'd refused. 'You're going to kill yourself on these slippery stones.'

I was getting tired by now and my knees were sore from trying to keep them bent at such an awkward angle. Besides, I was annoyed that Alice had ended up getting *my* stick. I wasn't in the mood for a lecture. I must have sounded impatient when I told her that.

'Fine. End up on a stretcher like that one,' she said, gesturing toward the team ahead of us. 'They'll be busy today with people like you running down the mountain as if you were teenagers.'

We walked together in silence as far as the saddle and a fresh crowd of pilgrims grazing through the snack kiosks. 'So what do you think of Croagh Patrick?' I asked Alice. 'Did you like the view?'

'County Mayo, God save us!' she said with a giggle. 'It looked more familiar to me up there than where we are down in Connemara. But I didn't really climb all the way to the top for the view, Steve.' She sounded serious now and I braced myself. 'And something else, while we're on the subject. You shouldn't have been so flippant with that girl and her confession. She's taking it all very seriously, you know.' I opened my mouth to protest, but Alice continued. 'Anyway this is the last time you'll be seeing her.' I held my breath. 'She'll be leaving soon on a quest of her own.' So Kathleen was about to cut short her stay . . . I knew she'd been disappointed with the course, having expected a lot more emphasis on Irish culture and less on the Irish language, but I had thought she'd hang around for at least a while longer.

'Maybe she'll head for Knock,' I said, trying to bait Alice with a reference to Ireland's home-grown version of Lourdes in the north-east of Mayo. For all I knew that's where she'd spent the morning. It seemed unlikely though, come to think of it. I'd only been there once and I didn't remember very much.

I turned to get Alice's reaction, but instead I saw Kate about to pass me on the trail. Her eyes widened. 'Are you talking to yourself again, Stiofáin?' she asked. 'We're getting a bit worried about you.' What did she mean 'again'? And who was this 'we' anyway? Maybe I'd better ask Alice to stop visiting me in such public places.

'Knock, knock, Kate. I was just remembering some of those old "knock, knock" jokes.'

'Such as?' she asked suspiciously.

Oh-oh. I had to think fast. 'Knock, knock,' I started.

Kate rolled her eyes. 'Okay, okay. Who's there?'

'Irish.'

'Iris who?'

'No, Kate, not Iris. *Irish.*'

There was a sigh. A testy one. 'Irish *who*?'

'Irish you'd let me in!' I said triumphantly.

Kate frowned and wrinkled her nose, as if a bad smell had just wafted under her delicate nostrils. 'That doesn't just stink, Stiofáin, it reeks.' She grabbed my arm and pulled me along. 'Hurry up. It's beginning to rain and we still have miles to go.'

By the time we reached the bottom of the mountain, we were soaked to the skin and the only place to shelter, a pub at the foot of the trail, was packed solid with pilgrims once again going astray on terra firma. I was about to make a crack to Kathleen about having been baptised as well as absolved of her sins on the holy Reek but thought the better of it. I'd be sure to hear about it later if I did.

We hadn't checked to see which way the wind was blowing the day we visited Inis Meáin (Inishmaan), the teardrop-shaped

'Middle Island' of the three Arans, but what was the point of consulting the weather forecast in Ireland? Summers here – and all the other seasons, too, come to think about it – were as unpredictable as love and next year's hottest Christmas toy. The boat ride over had been exhilarating for some, stomach-churning for others – I saw Morgan vomiting discreetly in a far-off corner of the ferry – and we were all drenched from the drizzle and the sea spray when we arrived at the small port looking out onto Foul Sound.

Absentmindedly I'd left the zipper partly open on my day pack and reached in to feel a sodden mass of maps, dictionary pages and a photograph of the class taken just a couple of days before. 'Don't you double-wrap all your gear in plastic bags when you pack?' asked Marsha, as neat and orderly as the gardens at Versailles and always dressed appropriately, come rain, shine or hurricane. 'When I get that organised, shoot me, will you?' I said crossly, wondering how long the papier-mâché that was now the contents of my bag would take to dry out in this climate – if it ever would at all.

I'd taken the bicycle along with me on the boat, thinking I might escape from the group and cycle along the *bóithríní*, or boreens, the narrow country lanes bordered by high stone walls that honeycomb Inishmaan. The wind and the rain deterred me from setting out and I joined the others, just rolling it alongside me. The island was smaller than I imagined it in any case, measuring just five kilometres in one direction and three in the other. It would be just as easy to walk.

We had a look at the thatched cottage where the playwright J.M. Synge had returned every autumn from 1898 to 1902 to learn Irish and listen to the legends and folk tales that would play such an important role in his dramas. Our only personal connection with the house was that our guide had been born there a half-century after Synge had left it forever; as far as we knew no student from the Áras Uí Chadhain had had the hots for the author of *The Playboy of the Western World* as yet. From the small window at the front of the cottage I could see Delores, a young Canadian student in the beginners' class, standing outside in the rain. She was dressed in a hooded woollen cloak that almost touched the ground and she held it up delicately with two pinched fingers, looking every bit the pre-Raphaelite Meryl Streep on the Cobb in *The French Lieutenant's Woman* as she surveyed the rocky terrain. Now *she* was a potential candidate.

Across the road from the cottage stood a massive stone fort erected almost 2000 years before on the edge of a narrow valley. The walls, built of tightly fitting rocks and stones, had been solid enough to support the trials of two millennia – including the prostrate Synge, who use to smoke and read in the sun here – so I hoisted myself to the top, circling the fort from above and looking across the bogland to the ocean. The sea was in such a rage it was sending columns of foam several metres into the air. It wasn't true what Tomás Ó Criomhthain had once said: 'The magic of the water is understood only by those who grew up on it.' Mike loved the ocean as much as I did and knew all about its magic. The problem was, like many people born inland, he didn't know to be frightened by it. I reached for the mobile phone and dialled his office number. He answered at once, but I don't think he could hear me and then the connection was lost.

Chris, who was always up for some adventure or mischief, had crossed over the road and joined me on the stone walls of the fort. 'Do you want to ride down to the cliffs over there?' I asked him, pointing to the west. 'Synge seemed to think they were pretty dramatic.' I pushed the bicycle to the top of the hill to get a rolling start, and Chris hopped on the back, sitting on one of the hooks on the elastic cords entwined around the luggage rack. 'Christ, that thing just pinched my butt!'

I laughed. 'You'd better be careful,' I told him. 'I've even got the bike trained.' Chris put his arms around my waist to balance himself. It felt familiar, holding and being held up. I missed that.

We coasted down the hill and, just as we neared the coast, rode straight into a hailstorm. Blinded by the ice, I skidded to a halt and we jumped off the bicycle, watching the white pellets form little piles against the grey stones and the russet soil. We weren't going to get very far in a storm – at least that was clear – and when we saw a man riding backward on a donkey approaching us, we decided it was time to head back to the pub where the others were undoubtedly taking shelter.

Our group had trebled the numbers of local clients, and the island's one and only pub was very busy for a weekday afternoon. 'The ice men cometh,' someone shouted as Chris and I ducked through the low door, our hair and eyelashes white with hail, to drip-dry in front of the turf fire ablaze on an August afternoon. Secure from the storm and fortified by the heat of the fire and the drink, before long people began to break into song without any kind of program, and just about everyone took their turn. We heard songs not only in Irish and English but in Greek, Catalan and Welsh as well. It was as *teolaí* a rainy afternoon as any I'd spent with Alice as a child, and with all the music and mirth I half-expected her to make an appearance.

I don't know why Alice stayed away that day; perhaps she could see I was busy and realised she wouldn't have my full attention. That was a pity. The afternoon on Inishmaan was the closest I ever came to feeling at home in the Gaeltacht, but even then I knew it wouldn't last. Alice must have recognised that too. She could see that I didn't know any of the words to the songs.

Things began to change for us in An Cheathrú Rua not long after that afternoon of song and camaraderie in the warm little pub on Inishmaan. It's difficult to pinpoint the exact time or cite a single event that caused the shift. One teacher – an Irishman who had made his home in the wind-blown flatlands of the Midwest, as different a world from his homeland as he could find – put it down to 'third-week syndrome', the period of the course when everyone started to get tired, fed up with the demands of intensive language learning and the routine. People grew irritable and bickered over minor things, things they would not have even noticed – much less mentioned – at the start. A competitive edge had also come into the picture as well; you could hear it in the way people were speaking. It said: 'My Irish is bigger than yours.'

In our house this tension led to a falling out between Marsha and Louise, an American woman from somewhere far south of the Mason–Dixon Line. She was a late arrival, having replaced Marcus who had returned to Germany after two weeks. He'd studied at the centre before and had registered for just half the course this time. Clearly he knew what to expect.

Louise spoke 'Erse', as she called it, with a drawl and demanded that we use it at all times and occasions, even to one another as we whispered privately in our rooms with the doors firmly closed. It was as if Éamon de Valera himself had risen from the grave and was determined to get it right with his charges this time.

At the beginning the decree sounded fair enough – we'd all come to Connemara to learn the language and this was a hurdle we'd all have to jump at some stage. As the week wore on, however, conversations began to flag among those of us whose vocabulary was still in its adolescence. There was only so much we could think to say about the weather and the choice of cereals in front of us on the breakfast table. We realised more than ever how much we'd all enjoyed being in a bilingual house. When Louise presented me with a ballpoint inscribed with the words *Ní scríobhann an peann seo ach Gaeilge* (This pen only writes in Irish), I began to worry that my dreams would become even more disordered than they'd been and that I'd never emerge from the maze.

My room in the house at Doire Fhatharta Mór couldn't accommodate much more than had already settled in there. Every square centimetre of space was accounted for by homework, guidebook corrections, my overly endowed suitcase and the complex and mysterious dreams that always seemed to descend on me whenever and wherever I slept in Ireland. Dreams about three-headed fish and people with holes in their hands . . . Dreams as convoluted as a Bulgarian opera, with characters – some familiar, many unknown – pole-vaulting from one setting and time frame into another. Memories jumbled together like a canister of lost buttons. Each morning I'd drag myself away from yet another instalment as the light began to seep through the mansard window and would sit, hunched over a cup of tea, trying to put the faces, the places, the episodes in any sort of order. But I usually gave up, surrendering myself to the labyrinth I knew I'd enter again that night. Eventually something would make sense.

One dream-saturated night I awoke and walked out into the hallway. The door to the bathroom was slightly ajar; I could see a ribbon of light on the carpet just outside. I pressed on the door and hit something solid. Whatever it was started scrambling about, making a sound on the floor like irritated fingers taps. Had Fluffy abandoned his watch outside the front door and found his way upstairs to lie on the cool tiles? That was unlikely. He was an outside dog with a job to do – one he took very seriously – nipping playfully at the heels of those he knew belonged in the house and barking ferociously at everyone else. I pushed the door open and saw Louise on the floor, gathering up her notes, tapes and dictionaries. 'I'm sorry. I couldn't turn the light on in my room to study,' she said. 'Otherwise I'd disturb Jen. It's all yours now.' Louise's resolve was sending her into every corner of the house. Nowhere was off-limits for the Gaelic now.

'Why don't you tape over the English words on the children's board games and write them out in Irish?' Louise asked Bridey one evening. The *bean an tí* looked dismayed. 'I'm not sure there is a word for "Twister" in Irish,' she said. 'And if there is, I don't know how to say it.'

These and a host of other irritations vexed us all but particularly Marsha, who had stayed with Bridey and Seán before and had expected to return to find things just the way they'd been in the past. 'Why should we be forced to do her bidding?' asked Marsha crossly. 'What right does she have to force something down our throats when everything was running so smoothly before?' The evening meals were consumed with sarcasm, angry stares and silences that were punctured only when Seán would remark on what the mechanic had told him he'd have to spend to get his second car back on the road again or how far he'd have to travel to deliver a consignment of furniture the next morning. I began to dread sitting down to dinner.

We were all trying to avoid taking sides, but it was an all-but-futile task when the forces were so clearly opposed and so powerful. No-one wanted to be on the losing side, but what was to be won? The easy way out was the door, and we'd excuse ourselves after dinner and shuffle back to the crowded comfort of our rooms alone. The dynamics of the great house in Doire Fhatharta Mór had changed, and I began to fear that we had too.

Apparently we weren't alone; there were problems at some of the houses where the other students were staying as well. No-one talked about them much, leaving them tethered to the door when they exited to walk along the road to the language centre. That would have been breaking confidence, laundering the dirty linen that Alice had always advised me not to do in public, and bringing shame to the 'family' and loss of face to themselves. The stories got around, nonetheless, circulated by the mailman, who would sit down at the kitchen table and recount what he'd heard on his run since the day before.

At first I didn't believe the tales, convinced that the quagmire of Doire Fhatharta Mór was unique. I'd always taken almost everything Liam had said with a generous amount of salt anyway. 'It's going to rain today,' he'd told me over a cup of tea one morning at the start of the course. 'How can you tell?' I asked him. 'Just look at the way the birds are hitting the ground there,' he said, pointing through the window to the field behind the house. 'That's a sure sign.' That day turned out to be one of the finest of our stay, bright and clear and not a single cloud obstructing the sun.

What he might have lacked in folk knowledge Liam surely made up for with a thorough grasp of gossip and if the rumours turned out to be true, things were going awry elsewhere as well. The *bean an tí* at Beth's house had turned on her, badgering her at every misstep – real or imagined. Beth hadn't turned the lights out in the hallway again, hadn't arrived for dinner at the appointed hour, hadn't answered her correctly in Irish. The woman even managed to provoke Brian too, as affable and accommodating a man as you'd encounter. One night she did a headcount as everyone slept, leaning over their creased and distant faces and sniffing, determined to unmask the culprit or culprits who had staggered home after closing time at An Chistin and failed to lock the front door behind them. Brian was furious and had apparently confronted her but we heard nothing further. The details remained within those four walls.

Members of the group began to spend less time at home, taking refuge in the pub, along the beach or on the trail that led to the Cnoc an Phobail (Hill of the People) that offered clear views in every direction, sometimes as far as the Cliffs of Moher in County Clare. We'd encounter one another in those places by chance, send out a greeting or remark on the weather, and move along in opposite directions. I began to wonder if I should bail out and head elsewhere – at least for a time.

One evening after dinner, Seán, his youngest son Caoimhín and I went out to fish in the bay off Lettermore in the Islands District that had once been Seán's home. He'd slow down to chat with almost everyone we passed on foot or in other cars along the narrow lanes; he seemed to know everyone and they knew him. When we reached the small dock in the bay, an old man loading the kelp that he'd harvested onto a raft loaned us his *currach*, which smelled of pitch and the fish it had carried to shore for decades or maybe even longer. Seán rowed with pieces of timber that resembled two-by-fours and I remarked that I'd never seen oars without blades. 'This is the way we've always done it here,' he said a little self-consciously. 'They'll get us where we need to go.'

After we'd transferred to Seán's motorboat and pumped out the bilge, a large gull flew over and settled on the bow, hitching a ride with us to the middle of the bay. 'Maybe he thinks we're going to catch his dinner for him,' said little Caoimhín, the Irish for Kevin. But the gull would have had to eat like a sparrow and not the albatross it was if it had relied on us for a meal. We threw down the anchor and the line and waited. And then waited some more. Nothing bit, nothing even nibbled. We changed our position in the current and tried again.

Eventually we brought up a small pollack that refused to give up the ghost. It thrashed around in the bottom of the boat, puffing up its gills and making an odd wheezing sound the likes of which I'd never heard from a fish. I was tempted to ask Seán to bring the creature's torture to an end and throw it back into the water, but Caoimhín beat me to it before I could open my mouth. 'You don't "catch" a fish in Irish,' Seán said, looking at me. 'You "murder" it.'

We stayed in the centre of the bay for a while, surrounded by islands and the hills of the mainland, saying nothing. It was a comfortable silence, one with no particular reason or purpose, and we sat listening to the waves strike gently against the sides of the boat. As the dusk settled in, we could see a man off in the distance raising lobster traps to check the day's catch and then dropping them back to the seafloor. Seán recognised the man as his brother, shouted a greeting to him and waved his hand. Once we'd pulled anchor, the current shoved us too close to his brother's boat, our fishing line tangling with one of the ropes attached to a lobster trap. We had to cut ours loose, dropping not just the line but the hook and sinker too.

'We're going to lose one of them,' said Seán out of the blue and nodded in the general direction of An Cheathrú Rua. I knew he wasn't talking about fishing tackle. 'I can probably guess which one.'

We headed towards shore, transferred back into the *currach* and rowed to the pier. Seán reached for the pollack and recoiled; it was still flapping when he threw it over to the seaweed harvester for lending us his boat. 'Sure he needs it more than we do,' he said. 'We wouldn't get much use of a fish like that.'

When we returned to the house at Doire Fhatharta Mór, Louise had gone, leaving behind nothing but a bin of crumpled paper and the musky scent of a perfume she liked to wear lingering in the bathroom. We might have been thinking about it but no-one asked after her or questioned where she'd gone. All of us – the other students, Bridey and Seán, even the kids – just seemed relieved to be back where we'd all started a few weeks before. For all we knew, she might have dived into the bay to hide out with those elusive schools of pollack; I wondered whether we'd all miss her just a bit once everything had returned to normal – if it ever could.

The next night Seán went out fishing on his own, leaving Caoimhín and I behind to play fetch with Fluffy away from the busy road in front. He returned with over a dozen pollack and just as many mackerel. We ate fish for the rest of the week.

Sometimes late in the afternoon after class and the usual checklist of activities, and almost always at the weekend, I'd explore the peninsula on my bicycle. Once or twice I even followed the road along the Bay of the Great Man and then through the Islands District as far as Leitir Mealláin (Lettermullen), seeking out the holy wells, tower ruins and ancient cemeteries so assiduously listed and described in the encyclopaedic guidebook I had bought in Galway. More often than not, though, I'd head south, away from the house, the language centre and the others, and pedal the few kilometres to the beach to lie in the soft sand and listen to the gulls call out overhead.

I'd abandoned Coral Beach to the tourists – it was well sign-posted and could easily be reached by car – not long after I'd discovered my own private spot. Trá an Tismeáin (Beach in the Middle) was on the southern coast of the peninsula, just beyond the small Loch an Dá Eala (Lake of the Two Swans) where I sought in vain for either of the regal birds each time I passed it.

The beach lay at the end of bogs and fields covered in wild-flowers and was almost always deserted, even in fine weather. Occasionally one or two visitors would stumble upon it as I had, but they stayed close to the path leading down to the beach and seldom ventured farther than the first outcrop of pointed rocks that split the Beach in the Middle into a series of small coves. In fact, when I did see a bather break away and swim towards me, or spot footprints of a beachcomber collecting shells along the tide-line, I'd feel disappointed, even resentful, as if I'd been discovered. Once I saw Kate walking in the field above me, looking out to sea, but I didn't shout out a greeting or gesture for her to come join me. The Beach in the Middle, or a small part of it anyway, was my world and I wanted to keep it that way.

I asked Bridey once why so few people visited what I considered to be the finest spot on the peninsula. She agreed that it was a peaceful place but seldom went there herself. 'That small paved area where you can park and turn a car around is new,' she said. 'Before they built that you had to back all the way out along the lane you'd come in on. No-one seems to know about the change.'

My preferred 'seat' at the Beach in the Middle was a large flat rock jutting out from the sand at a comfortable angle. I could sit down and lean against it, watching the gulls and the occasional cormorant alight from the rocks close to the shore, swoop down and murder fish. On the horizon were the dark outlines of the Aran Islands, closely linked with, but still a world apart from, where I was in Connemara.

The shore was usually covered in seaweed, brown kelp and different types of dried wrack that popped when I stepped on them. I'd done the same thing when I was a child on the opposite coast thousands of kilometres to the west. In fact, this could have been any beach in New England, with limpets holding fast to the wet rocks, brittle shells of razor clams littering the shore and horseshoe crabs dragging themselves ungainly to and from the water.

The horseshoe crabs were primitive-looking things and frightening too, with their suit of armour and long spike attached to the back. Sometimes they'd be turned upside-down by the wash and deposited on the sand, their undersides exposed to the sky, and unable to right themselves. I wondered whether I should flip them over before they dried out in the sun, cracking and splitting like old lacquer, or whether that would be interfering with some great Darwinesque scheme. I would watch the spidery legs making those pointless pedalling motions for as long as I could bear it and then would push them over with my toe or a stick. Survival of the fittest be damned.

Alice was all for this rescue operation – she almost burst into tears when she saw the first of these walking helmets the wrong way up – and she enjoyed watching me pop the wrack's air sacs, pretending to be startled whenever I did it near her. The Beach in the Middle was as comfortable and familiar a spot for her as it was for me and she often joined me there, taking my stony seat and letting me lean against her. We had some of our best times there, chatting away about new things and reminiscing about relatives and old places.

She told me stories about her childhood that I hadn't heard before or possibly just didn't remember, like how she helped her father cap the bottles of beer that he brewed in the cellar on Sedalia Road during Prohibition and the time her mother crept up behind her and cut off the braid that hung down to the small of her back. 'She thought long hair was for girls and not for young women,' she explained when I asked why Nellie, virtually canonised in our family's panoply of departed souls, would have done such a thing. 'And I was coming of age.'

Alice also talked about her one and only love, a shipping clerk called Jimmy McDonough who had courted her passionately and then walked away one fine day, leaving her with the words 'I think we should call it quits, Alice' to ponder and analyse for days and weeks and months and maybe even a lifetime. I didn't know whether there had been any other men in her life – a passing fancy, a kiss borrowed at an office Christmas party, even the excitement of smelling a certain Mr So-and-So's aftershave as he passed in the corridor.

Wasn't there a man called Bob Willoughby who would escort me around when I'd visit her as a child – all dressed up in a coat and bow tie and looking every bit a midget Beau Brummel – at the bank downtown where she worked? 'Oh, that Bob Willoughby is full of malarkey, isn't he?' she'd say as we ate hot fudge sundaes at the Brigham's ice-cream parlour on Tremont Street. She'd always have a smile on her face when she said it.

I heard Alice sniffle and turned to her. She looked away though I could see her cheek was wet. 'Are you feeling "meeyeh"?' I asked her gently, surprised at being able to resurrect a word I hadn't used or heard in years. 'Meeyeh' was what Alice said for feeling out of sorts or unwell. Was it the same as the Irish *mí-ádh* for 'misfortune' or 'out of luck', another word that had survived, somewhat twisted and misshapen, through the generations? I didn't know how to ask her about Bob Willoughby and all those things. Besides, it was really none of my business.

With the options available to her in An Cheathrú Rua so limited, Alice may have just enjoyed the Beach in the Middle by default. She gave Coral Beach a wide berth unless we stayed close to the shore, which was impossible on my bicycle, and I could never get her to visit the eastern side of the peninsula. There was a strand there too, just below the cemetery where the Great Blasket writer Muiris Ó Súileabháin had been buried after drowning off the coast a half-century before. It was called Trá na Reilige, or Graveyard Beach.

The beginners' class had visited the cemetery one sunny afternoon with their teacher, who was a big fan of the author of *Twenty Years A-Growing*. Yuko, a Japanese student with whom I'd become friendly, told me about the excursion, and I asked her whether she'd been swimming at the beach. 'Oh, no,' she giggled self-consciously, covering her mouth with her right hand. 'I'm afraid to drown there.' She knew I understood her. Cemeteries always gave people the willies in Japan, as much by day as by night. It was the same in Hong Kong. Flats that happened to face a graveyard – however far away – would go for half-price or be sold to *gwei-los*, 'ghost people' as we foreigners were known, who didn't seem to notice or care.

The ruins of a medieval chapel were close to the beach, and one day I suggested to Alice that we go down and have a look. 'Oh, I won't be going down there with you,' said Alice. 'Not in a million years.' Which of course she probably had ahead of her, but I wasn't going to get any joy or *scéal* on *that* score. Forever and a day – at least that's what I think the Baltimore Catechism told us. Or something like that anyway.

'Now wait just a minute,' I said. 'This "graveyard-by-the-sea" business is an Asian thing. It's got nothing to do with us here in Connemara. That conversation I had with Yuko . . .' But Alice was rocking on her heels with her arms folded in front of her and not listening to me. 'You keep trying to drag me to places I don't want to go to and see things I shouldn't,' she said. 'This isn't your home now and it's certainly not mine. Maybe I'll just give you awhile to think about that and not waste your time standing here talking to me.'

I started to protest, to tell her that we could go to the Beach in the Middle instead. I wanted to assure her too that I never considered our conversations a waste of time. Where would I be, where would she be without them? But Alice began to make a high-pitched wailing sound, a hair-raising keening that would spook a *bean sí*, a 'fairy woman' or 'banshee'. 'Do you mean to tell me that's what you expect to hear over there?' I asked her. But I'd turned to the east and she had headed west so I went down the road on my own.

Graveyard Beach was not a very attractive place, it has to be said. It was small and crowded, with coarse sand and views across to Ros an Mhíl (Rossaveal), where the ferries departed for the Aran Islands. It wasn't a patch on the Beach in the Middle but then what other spot on the peninsula was? Still, there was the graveyard to explore and a host of Irish words on the stones to try to recognise and learn: 'age', 'year', 'soul', 'memory', 'God's hands'. They'd all come in useful at some stage, I supposed.

On a small rise facing the sea were the remains of the little church, thought to be the oldest structure in An Cheathrú Rua. Given that almost everything else man-made on the peninsula looked like it had been born, well, maybe not yesterday but a couple of days before, I wouldn't want to dispute that claim. Wherever it ranked in the age hierarchy, it was the oldest thing I'd seen for a while.

The four walls of the church were intact, but the roof had disappeared; judging from all the vegetation within and the rain damage to the walls, that had happened a long time before. At the entrance to what was once the porch there was a large trough, a holy water font maybe, and on the ground to the east the pieces of a stone ogee window frame.

I myself didn't hear anything in the chapel, beyond the occasional cry of a gull following one of the boats that were heading out of Rossaveal and the hissing of the wind through the chinks in the stone walls, but somehow I knew Alice was close by. I leaned against the chancel wall and thought some more about what she'd said: 'This isn't your home now and it's certainly not mine.'

'So where is home then, Alice? You seem to have all the answers. If this church, this peninsula or this country isn't home, where will I find it? On an outlying island in Hong Kong, the top of Gellért Hill in Budapest, the backstreets of East London? Help me with this one, Al. *Cabhraigh liom.*'

In the centre of the chapel was a large clump of montbretia, an invasive plant that thrives anywhere it can gain purchase in the acid, peaty soil of Connemara. Its bright orange blossoms, arranged like a zigzag atop long, fragile-looking stalks, began to flutter in the wind and it looked for a moment as if the chapel shell was on fire – a flame ephemeral, yet timeless. This was a fire that would burn in a ruined church in a corner of Connemara for a long time.

Any of those places I'd mentioned to Alice – any place at all, in fact – could be home now, again or in the future. One thing was certain, though: I'd never be home alone.

Chapter VIII

The Gaeltacht

If you were to look at a map of Ireland dating from the early nineteenth century that had been shaded to show the areas in which Irish was spoken as a first language and then compared it with one marking today's *Gaeltachtaí*, or Gaeltachts, you would be shocked to see to what extent the language has lost ground over the past two hundred years.

The map from two centuries ago would incorporate more than two-thirds of the island of Ireland, representing some 2.4 million people. On the more recent map there would be just a dozen small smudges in seven areas, ranging in size from small to minuscule and strewn mostly along the west coast. Some 86,000 people live in the Gaeltacht today, the majority of them – just over 70 per cent – Irish-speakers but, according to the most recent census in 1996, only 21,000 adults there speak Irish on a daily basis. Non-Irish speakers live in the Gaeltacht, of course, and not all schools there teach in Irish.

The Gaeltacht, a term that is used to refer to all the Irish-speaking districts collectively or just a single one, is not the only place where Irish is spoken regularly in Ireland, of course; if that were the case, the language would have died out long ago or, at best, be about to give up the ghost. Irish can be heard spoken with as much aplomb and enthusiasm in places as diverse as banks in Dublin, community centres in Belfast and pubs in Cork City.

While more than 1.43 million people in the Irish Republic claim to have an ability to speak the language, approximately 50,000 adults outside the borders, as they were drawn up in 1956 and adjusted later, say they use it every day of their lives. This area outside the Gaeltacht – that is, most of Ireland – is called the Galltacht, which comes from the historical Irish word *gall*. The term has been used to identify everyone from the Gauls and the Norsemen to the Anglo-Normans. In effect, it means 'foreigner'.

The Gaeltacht is, however, the last bastion where Irish is spoken as a community language, where ordering a pint, buying a newspaper or eavesdropping on someone else's conversation *as Gaeilge* is as natural as rain, which is just about anytime in this Atlantic climate. The Gaeltacht is where the language can be allowed to grow and develop and, at the same time, where it can be protected.

These natural environments of a language that stretches back some 2500 years are thus important to a state that, at least officially, encourages the development of bilingualism among all its citizens. Think of the various Gaeltachts as having the right kind of soil and the optimum climate for a certain crop you want to grow. To language activists they are even more. They are treasures, 'holy' sites to which they make pilgrimages and drink at the fountain of history and fluency. The image is not so very different for Irish-language students at any level, I suppose. We've all done the same thing to a greater or lesser extent at some time or other.

The Gaeltachts range in size and population from the Gaillimh (Galway, also known as Connemara) and Dún na nGall (Donegal) Gaeltachts in the west and north-west with about 34,000 and 24,000 people respectively to a tiny though active one in Mí (Meath), near Dublin, with about 1400 people. Others are in Counties Maigh Eo (Mayo), Ciarraí (Kerry), Corchaigh (Cork) and Port Láirge (Waterford).

I'd been to all of the Gaeltachts before for one reason or another – on assignment, in search of a castle or ruin, just passing through. Now, with the situation still uneasy in An Cheathrú Rua, I decided to take a break from the silences and the stares and visit them again. But I would be entering from a different door this time. With a smattering of Irish and the familiarity of a '*Dia duit*' tossed to a passer-by and bounced back to me, would they look and feel the same?

In *Out of Africa* Karen Blixen had mused: 'If I know a song of Africa . . . does Africa know a song of me?' I wondered the same thing before I set out on my journey. I'd arrive with a limited glossary and a few verb conjugations to fit awkwardly into a question if I wanted or needed something, and I'd surely leave with a lot more than I'd come with. But would I only be taking things away? If I were to drop a word, a phrase, a sentence at each place where I stopped, would I leave behind anything of myself too? If I could carry away with me pleasantries exchanged, a shop assistant's help, a young boy's dizzying set of directions, would it go the other way? Would the Gaeltacht recognise the little rental car I drove or my bicycle as I sped along a country lane? Would it see the bottle of water I'd drunk from on a warm afternoon, the indent of the mattress on which I'd slept?

Perhaps it might, even on such a short escape. Mine was a world of surfacing then, not coming from the bottom up but staying at the top and looking down. There would be plenty and hear along the way but not much time. I still had lots of lessons ahead of me and there was homework to do too.

The Waterford Gaeltacht, some sixty kilometres from the county seat of Waterford City, occupies part of a bird-shaped peninsula that appears on the map to be pecking at Dungarvan Bay. It is what they call a 'Breac-Ghaeltacht', a 'speckled Gaeltacht' of mixed English and Irish-speaking communities, and only one-third of the adults among its 1200 inhabitants speak Irish regularly. But its Irish-language college in the main town of An Rinn (Ring) attracts students from all over the country. Perhaps they'd have something to say.

I stayed at a *leaba agus bricfeasta* called Aisling, not exactly the 'vision' its name suggested but comfortable enough with views across the bay to the foot of the Monavullagh Mountains. I had hardly been expecting the Ritz – this was a simple B&B after all – but when I rang the doorbell the young man who answered was dressed in a tuxedo. I looked at him curiously and he laughed. 'I'll get my Mum,' he said. The proprietor and I fumbled a bit in Irish, but the Munster dialect spoken around Ring is said to be the most conservative (read: difficult) in Ireland and she was anxious to tell me about her daughter studying in Pennsylvania, not to mention why her son was dressed in formal attire. 'He's off to the debs tonight,' she said in English, apparently to some sort of prom, and then called to him over my shoulder. 'Behave yourself, won't you?' she admonished rather than asked him. 'And bring your date home at a decent hour.'

The owner of An Carn, a charming but disconcertingly empty restaurant on a hill high above the sea, told me that the college's summer course had ended and Ring felt deserted as a result. He was a local, an Irish-speaker who had learned the chef's trade in Dublin and had returned home to open his own restaurant. He advised me to go to Mooney's, a pub at the bottom of the hill, where I'd hear a lot of the language spoken. 'It's Thursday,' he said. 'There's a session on, and they'll all be coming out tonight.'

Mooney's counted just a few more clients than An Carn when I first entered and the barman had ample time to chat. 'Lots of people speak Irish around here,' he said. 'They all do.' But as the door opened and closed and the numbers of people at the bar swelled, all I could hear around me were exclamations in Dublinese about bogeys and eagles and near holes-in-one. Most of the blow-ins were strays from one of several golf courses in the area and they were anxious to tee off at their favourite nineteenth hole. Then the musicians arrived, two guitarists and a banjo player who began plucking out 'Red River Valley'. I bolted, leaving a cigarette smouldering in the ashtray.

The road to a settlement called An Seanphobal (The Old Parish) ran across a flat stretch of land inland from the coast and past conifers, a few lonely farmhouses and a sign pointing the way to a megalithic tomb. Some of the road signs were in Irish – *Géill slí* (Give way) and *Stad* (Stop) – but estate agents in Ring must have been seeking English-speaking homebuyers, judging from all the 'For Sale' signs around, and the Waterford County

Council preferred the language of authority to get its point across. 'Persons Found Dumping Refuse Here Will be Prosecuted' a sign read in English only, to make sure everyone got the message.

I was out of the Waterford Gaeltacht as quickly as I'd entered it and heading for Ardmore, a beach town of caravan camps, holiday homes and a tall medieval oratory pointing like an indignant finger toward heaven.

Bordering Waterford to the west is the large county of Cork. Its Gaeltacht is divided in two: Múscraí (Muskerry) a series of villages in a wooded valley lying halfway between Cork City and Killarney, and tiny Oileán Chléire (Clear Island) off the coast of West Cork. The tourist blight and the flocks of whitecaps gambolling towards the shoreline at Ardmore had put me off the sea for awhile, so I headed inland for the cool hills, through the tumult of the republic's second-largest city and past what the good-humoured citizens of Cork call the 'Four-faced Liar', the tower above Saint Anne's Church in Shandon with clocks facing in each direction. Each of them tells a different time.

The city traffic was just about to release me from its jaws and disgorge me back onto the road heading west when I heard a voice say 'Let's go to Fermoy'. I recognised the name of that town immediately: my maternal grandmother – and you-know-whose mother – was born there. 'That's forty kilometres north of here, and we're travelling west,' I told Alice. 'Besides, we don't know anyone in Fermoy or even where Nellie lived for that matter.' I didn't know what to call a grandmother I'd never had the chance to meet. A first name sounded a bit too familiar for someone who would have been at least six *scór* years by then, but I couldn't think of anything else.

'What's that in miles from Cork?' Alice asked, pronouncing it like 'cock' in true Bostonian. I refused to get drawn into that one – twenty-five miles would only make Fermoy sound that much closer. I tried not to think about it for awhile, with only partial success.

'Then what about Blarney Castle? I want to kiss the stone!'

I was about to ask my loquacious aunt what made her think she needed any more of the gab than she already had, but I kept my mouth shut. Poor Alice. I had been dragging her around to places in Ireland that she didn't know or care about since we first met up in Dublin. I could tell she hadn't really put her mind to the Gaelic and probably never would. Now she was back – 'Saints be praised!' as she liked to say – and wanted to see the Ireland she always dreamed and sang about. The real Ireland, as far as she was concerned. Blarney was just up the road anyway; I could see it signposted off the roundabout we were about to enter. I couldn't deny Al Blarney.

I'd never really been there myself. Well, in a way I had. I'd covered it while updating one of the editions of the guidebook. I'd gone there, of course, and spoken with the staff, asking all the usual questions and checking the perishable information: opening times, admission fees, discounts for students with and without national IDs, access for the handicapped. I didn't even consider joining the crowds and following them inside for the climb to the top of the tower house, over to the nineteenth-century baronial mansion next door full of Victorian trappings and chandeliers made of Waterford glass or – perish the thought! – to the giant tourist shop selling everything from woollen garments to tacky green telephones in the shape of Ireland accompanied by a 'No Blarney' guarantee.

'You're a hot ticket!' Alice cried as I took the turn for Blarney. She was getting giddy and quickly pulled down the visor in front of her and glanced into the small mirror. 'Look at the state of me! I look like who began it,' she said. I couldn't help myself. 'And ran!' I shouted. I never did understand what that expression of hers meant but I could still finish it for her. She was fishing around in her oversized pocketbook and would soon begin working her compact of pink face powder and tube of deep red lipstick overtime.

We were in Blarney in no time. And you know what? We loved it, both of us: the tower, the narrow spiral staircase, bending over backwards and planting our lips on the cold, grey stone.

We didn't stop talking and laughing about it till we reached Muskerry, especially about the fat German man shouting *Scheisse!* when all the change poured out of his pockets, jingling and clinking as it fell into the pit far below.

Muskerry is another Breac-Ghaeltacht, with a scattered population of about 3000 and has only one small district where Irish is spoken by more than half the adults every day. Two of its half-dozen settlements – Baile Bhuirne (Ballyvourney) and Baile Mhic Íre (Ballymakeera) – are on the main Cork–Killarney highway and look like any roadside towns you'd pass along the way in Ireland and never give a second thought to. To the south of the highway, it's a different world in the isolated glens and the valley of the River Lee and that's where I made my turn.

I passed no real towns as I travelled along the cool and shady road, just the occasional house. When several bunched together, the clump merited an uninspired name like Ré na nDoirí (Renanaree), meaning 'grove row', and even a post office. I'd heard that the quality of the land and enough jobs in the area's small industries to keep the population employed had made this one of the wealthiest Gaeltachts. Some of the houses looked quite grand, with their trimmed lawns and tidy gardens, and the cars in the driveways were new. One of the small companies I passed was in the business of making garden sheds and was supported, a sign announced proudly, by Údarás na Gaeltachta, the Gaeltacht Authority.

Béal Átha an Ghaorthaidh (Ballingeary), on the banks of the River Lee, seemed an attractive village, with modern pastel-coloured bungalows and a famous *coláiste samhradh* (summer college) for Irish-language students. I could see everything there was to see by turning my head to the left and then the right; there was little to detain me here but the buzzing of the bees, maybe, or the laughter of the Lee as it tumbled over the tickling stones of the riverbed. I was thirsty. A shop called Ó Corcora promised, among other things, *earraí feirme*, farm goods. At least there might be a trough of some sort.

'*Ba mhaith liom buidéal uisce, más é do thoil é*,' I repeated to myself and then barked out my request for a bottle of water to the shop assistant before the door had time to swing shut behind me. The woman at the counter looked up at me startled and went to fetch one. 'You're not from here,' she said and I agreed that 'the right was at her'. '*Is as Boston tú* (You're from Boston).' She repeated it slowly, skimming over what I'd just told her before she opened the floodgates. 'Were you not born in Ireland? Why are you learning the Irish? That's sixty-five *pingin* for the water. Oh, I wouldn't be understanding Connemara Irish now. We have a much softer Irish here. The children come to learn it at the college, you know. It's a crazy place when they're all here . . .' The only thing I left behind in Ballingeary was my empty water bottle in the bin outside Ó Corcora. There didn't seem to be much room for anything else.

I climbed back up the hill and past the trail leading to Gugán Barra (Gougane Barra), site of a mountain lake and erstwhile home of Finbarr, the patron saint of Cork. This was not the time for that sort of pilgrimage. Instead, I followed a narrow, winding road across the hills and coasted down to the village of Cúil Aodha (Coolea), where the late musician and composer Seán Ó Riada had lived and had once described as an area where English was spoken in one house and Irish in another. A pamphlet I'd picked up along the way promised 'a well-spring of all that is best in Irish music and the Irish language' but all I could hear was the bleating of sheep and the hollow clang of a cowbell up on the hillside. It was tea time in rural Ireland.

The overly generous borders of the Kerry Gaeltacht include parts of the Uíbh Ráthach (Iveragh Peninsula) which, as anyone on a coach tour of the Emerald Isle can tell you, is where you'll find the Ring of Kerry. I ignored Alice's protests and drove straight past Killoorglin, the springboard for the tour buses that follow the route as mindlessly as mill horses, and headed north for the Corca Dhuibhne (Dingle Peninsula).

The 'real' Kerry Gaeltacht had caught my imagination. Its centre, An Daingean (Dingle), with a mere 1500 people, is the largest conurbation of any Gaeltacht in Ireland. And then there were Na Blascaodaí (The Blaskets), six islands in the Atlantic – in particular An Blascaod Mór (The Great Blasket) – that spawned a generation of Gaeltacht writers. It was their tales and stories had helped to kick-start modern Irish literature in the twentieth century.

What I didn't know was that a music festival – a *big* music festival – was descending on Dingle for the weekend, filling the pubs, the restaurants and virtually every bed in town to capacity. 'Some guidebook writer, you are,' Alice teased as I tramped the streets, knocking on the door of any house that had a B&B sign out front, and even a few that didn't.

Even after I'd managed to stash my bag in the tiny room of a B&B overlooking Dingle Harbour (for which I'd paid twice as much – in advance – as I should have), my luck stayed on the same course. A small, earnest-looking crowd was gathered around a middle-aged woman with dark curly hair and cherubic cheeks outside An Café Liteartha, an Irish-language bookshop-cum-café on Dykegate Street. A poster in the window invited *Gaeilgeoirí* – well, it was only in Irish so I assumed only Irish speakers were expected – to hear the poet Biddy Jenkinson read from her work between the hours of six and seven that evening. I'd tried to read Jenkinson's *Uiscí Beatha* (*Waters of Life*) without much success; I had even thought the title meant *Whiskeys*. It was quarter past seven anyway.

Music of all kinds – from trad and folk to jazz and rock – had started seeping through the doors and the windows of the pubs lining Main Street, and An Droichead Beag (The Little Bridge) at the bottom of the road promised a particularly heavy *seisiún cheoil* (music session) that night. The young bar staff, their numbers inflated to cope with all the festival-goers, were joking and teasing one another in an Irish that sounded more like the DIY tapes I'd listened to at home than what I'd heard in Connemara. 'We're from over the bridge,' one of them told me when I asked him if they all lived in Dingle. 'From Dún Chaoin.'

I recognised the name of the settlement on the western tip of the peninsula. Dún Chaoin (Dunquin) is a 'Fíor-Ghaeltacht', a 'true Gaeltacht', one where more than 80 per cent of adults speak Irish as their first language. They're rare enclaves these days and are only found in Kerry, Connemara and Donegal. I'd be on my way there early the next morning.

In Foxy Johns, an ancient hybrid of a place with a bar on one side of a narrow room and a hardware counter on the other, I chatted with a psychologist from Brisbane who was on her own quest. Mandy was searching for the perfect squeeze-box and wouldn't even consider anything without leather stops. I was relieved when she told me exactly what it was that she was looking for without having to ask. I'd imagined something kinkier than a little button accordion.

Mandy had developed a strong interest in Irish music and had taught herself to play in no time, though her family hadn't been particularly disposed to music of any kind and her Irish ancestry went back five generations. I told her about racial memory, but she was a scientist not a philosopher and didn't want to open the door to that idea even for a moment. In fact, she looked at me as if I were mad. 'There's someone waving at you,' she said and pointed over my shoulder, visibly relieved to be able to distract my attention and probably flee.

I froze and looked anxiously across to the display racks of hand and power tools, cases of nuts, bolts and screws. Behind the counter was a sextet of musicians fiddling with their instruments. Their combined age could have taken us all back to the time the Ulster earls flew the coop, which was why Georgia Dave stood out.

Dave was a student I knew from An Cheathrú Rua, a gangling young guy of about twenty, all arms and legs and a wide, toothy grin. I liked Dave; he must have been on the lam too. He had sat down among the musicians, and I leaned over the counter to talk to him, knocking over a pair of pliers and a monkey wrench in the process. 'What are you doing here, G.D.?' I asked him.

He held up a pair of spoons and gave me a *miongháire* (half-laugh), the lovely way to say 'smile' in Irish. 'I guess I gotta start somewhere,' he drawled. A natural musician, Dave could pick up an instrument he'd never played before and make it perform for him; I'd seen him do it one rainy afternoon in a shop over in Cloch na Rón (Roundstone) with a kind of drum made of goatskin called a *bodhrán*, a small accordion (well, a squeeze-box as I now knew it was called) and a penny whistle. He was on a tour of the Gaeltacht too, part of a university degree project, and was determined to play as many sessions and venues as he could along the way. Surrounded by such talent in Dingle, he probably wasn't doing too badly with the spoons as his first ticket to play. Such a versatile instrument, so easily transported too.

The wind, the rain and the *craic* of the spoons and other amusements the night before kept me under the sheets longer than I'd intended, and before my eyes had prised themselves fully open I was across the Milltown Bridge in the Fíor-Ghaeltacht and careening past the peninsula's embarrassment of ancient forts, oratories, *clocháin* (beehive cells) and ogham stones. If I didn't reach Dunquin in time to catch the ferry to the Great Blasket I wouldn't get there at all. A man was looking down from the car park to the narrow pier far below when I pulled up. 'The boat's about to go,' he shouted. 'Can you make it down in two minutes?'

I ran for the steep path that led down to the pier and spotted Mandy at the edge of the bluff, looking rather forlornly out across the sea to the island. 'Aren't you coming along?' I called out to her. She shook her head. 'I'm afraid of the ocean,' she said. From Brisbane? Afraid of the sea? 'That's the Pacific,' she said. 'Peaceful, remember?' The Pacific I remembered was a sea of typhoons and waves that bobbed up and down. Maybe things were calmer off Queensland. I'd make a mental note of that and ask Mike one day.

Mandy had made the right decision to jump ship before she'd even boarded; she would not have liked the trip. Not one bit. The waves buffeted the small boat violently as we crossed the sound, causing it to rock and list and me to start getting worried. Before we reached the middle of the channel, Alice had me casting my eyes around for the lifejackets, craning to see whether they had the complicated straps I could never seem to manage to do up. The handful of other passengers who had slid down the path ahead of me didn't appear fazed by Neptune's horseplay. Maybe they were sailors. They might just have been British.

It would be difficult to imagine any place in the Gaeltacht as striking or evocative as the Great Blasket. The island rose gradually from the east like a wedge, with jagged cliffs plunging down to the sea on the three other sides. It looked old and scarred now, tired of battling the storms and the waves on its own. The foundations of a couple of dozen houses and farm buildings were the only reminders that it once had help in its struggles.

The Great Blasket of less than a century before was a different world altogether, a lively community of 160 people who fished, carried turf down from the top of the hills, chose their own island king and dreamed their dreams in Irish. Perhaps it wasn't so different from how island-dwellers lived in other Gaeltachts, but it was a story that had never been told before. When Irish-language enthusiasts from the outside, among them the Norwegian Carl Marstrander and the Briton Robin Flower, visited the island, local people were encouraged to write their own stories in their own way. From them emerged highly individualistic records of the island and its culture.

These autobiographies and recollections would prove to be a blessing, both to Irish literature and the nation's history. By the end of World War II, emigration and death had reduced the population of the Great Blasket by two-thirds and only fifteen houses remained occupied. Most of the people still there were too old or too young to support themselves; the mainstay had been drift-netting for mackerel which meant carrying the catch by boat to Dunquin, loading it onto a donkey for the journey up the hill and then by horse and buggy to Dingle to sell it in the market. When bad weather prevented boats from bringing in supplies and a young man died for lack of medical treatment, the government offered to relocate the fifty or so remaining residents elsewhere. In 1953 the island was abandoned.

As we approached the shore in an inflatable dinghy, the only signs of life were the flocks of sheep dotting the green hills and turf smoke curling up from the only two buildings still standing on the island. I asked Fergal, the boatman, what they were. 'The one just ahead is a hostel,' he said, 'and that one to the south is where I live.' He had pointed to a red and white, solid-looking house, one that would put up a decent fight in any struggle with the wind and the rain.

I asked him whether it wasn't a lonely existence, living on an abandoned island. 'Oh, it's not as bad as you'd think,' he said. 'We get quite a walking crowd and sightseers here when the weather is fine. Relatives of the old families are always coming back too. Some of the Sayers brood from Springfield, Massachusetts, were here just the other day.' The Great Blasket lived on somehow, attracting the energetic, the curious, people with memories.

Alice refused to get off the boat anchored offshore, mumbling something about 'not awakening the ghosts keening on the paths', so I walked alone to what was once Bóthar Nua, the 'New Road', now overgrown and punched with little 'Vs' from the hoofs of the sheep that raced skittishly ahead of me. At the top of the hill, I played the same game the young Muiris Ó Súileabháin did when he tried to locate his house from here with his grandfather in *Twenty Years A-Growing*, but there wasn't much left to identify. The signal tower, which marked the end of the road, still stood, and the hostel, one of several slate-roofed houses that the government had built for the islanders in 1909, was where the celebrated *sianachaí* Peig Sayers had told her stories. To the north-east was the Trá Bhán (White Strand) where Tomás Ó Criomhthain did battle with the giant seal and almost lost his leg in doing so. The strand had always been lively, the place where the islanders gathered to welcome incoming supply boats or a new teacher and the men played violent games of hurley at Christmas. Now it was just a deserted beach washed over by the surf.

When I came back down the hill I met a group of men in wet suits running up the track from the shore towards the hostel. They'd been diving just offshore and one of their number, inexperienced and apparently suffering the effects of a night on the town in Dingle, had panicked, rising to the surface too quickly. He was lucky, the dive master said, he wasn't in any real danger, but the sea was too rough to take him back by boat. They were trying to summon an emergency helicopter. The diver lay on a blanket on the rocks close to where the dinghy had docked. His face was the white of a flounder's belly and his eyes darted around nervously as he sucked oxygen from a portable tank.

I returned to Dingle via the peninsula's northern coast, stopping first at the Blasket Centre to catch a glimpse of how the island looked in its glory days – a living, breathing entity and not just a place where people came to gawk, remember or almost kill themselves. The faces staring back at me from all the old photographs on the walls were gone now, most of them dead and the rest scattered to the four winds. The likes of them would never be again, as Tomás Ó Criomhthain had mused at the end of *The Islandman*, and that was certain. They'd be a different kind of people now, adapted to a new time and culture, fighting not storms and giant seals but other tempests and different monsters. There would still be stories to tell. There would always be plenty of those.

Ballyferriter, another Irish-speaking enclave on the peninsula, was just down the road, a pretty little village with brightly painted houses, a handful of music pubs, a small museum devoted to the history and culture the peninsula and, of all incongruous things, a shop selling lampshades. I spotted a small grocer's and pulled over to the kerb.

'*Agus fiche Benson, más é do thoil é* (And twenty Bensons, please),' I asked the shop assistant as I dropped my bottle of water, bananas and a copy of the *Irish Times* on the counter.

She handed me two packets and I looked at her quizzically, repeating what I'd said. 'Aren't there ten in each box?' she asked me. I explained that the smaller packets contained ten cigarettes, the larger ones twenty.

'*Gabh mo leithscéal* (Accept my half-story),' she said, in that fetching way people apologise in Irish. What could be more unfortunate than a half-story for a race of people who lived not to eat but to tell a tale? 'It's my first week on the *jab*.'

I carried on through other villages, where I heard more Irish around me, exchanged a few pleasantries and went as far as Cuas an Bhodaigh (Brandon Creek), from where Saint Brendan was supposed to have set out in a coracle of wood and leather on his voyage of discovery to America some eight centuries before Columbus. But what I'd left behind in the shop at Ballyferriter was my best offering on the Dingle Peninsula.

Often when I'd leave the Gaeltacht and re-enter English-speaking Ireland it would feel as though I'd exchanged one world for another. Everything seemed different, not just the road signs and the intonation of the voices around me, but the faces of people in grocery stores, the interiors of pubs, even the sound of the sea. Most Irish speakers told me that this was not their impression, that it was all the same Ireland – Gaeltacht or Galltacht – and they just laid the Irish aside temporarily.

'Sure the *craic* is different in Irish than in English,' a *Gaeilgeoir* visiting Galway from one of the Gaeltachts told me, 'just like a whiskey high is different from a Guinness one.' And then, as if sharing a confidence, he said, 'Maybe it's better.' He'd just have to wait until he got home for that.

I felt comfortable as I walked through the streets of Galway, as if I were back in the home of an old friend, familiar but full of enough surprises and new things to be forever interesting. In many ways I was. Mary Sexton gave me an effusive *fáilte* as always and Donal quizzed me about the course when he'd returned from church. I was lucky in Galway too. I found a copy of a book I'd wanted for ages and attended a talk given by a popular Irish historian at Dubray's Bookshop in the evening. Of course everything was in English again. I'd put the Gaeltacht to the side for a moment, and that was comfortable and familiar too.

I was heading down High Street after the talk, trying to decide what to do for what little remained of the evening, when someone called out from behind, trying to get my attention. I turned around and recognised the man who had been sitting next to me at Dubray's. 'Fancy a pint?' he asked. I looked at him not with suspicion but surprise; we hadn't exchanged a word at the talk. 'Don't be worrying yourself,' he said. 'I'm not gay.' I told him that I wasn't concerned in the least but that he might be. 'Fair play,' he said and laughed. 'Got that sorted.' Ó Neachtain's, Galway's favourite time-warp trad pub, was just in front of us so we breathed our last of the cool night air and entered.

Paddy was curious why I'd asked the historian his impressions about the attitudes of the Irish towards their overseas cousins and the state of the Irish language in the north today. 'Are you a journalist?' he asked. I told him about the course in Connemara and he told me he spoke seven languages, including the Irish he learned in school. He'd travelled quite a bit in Europe, Asia and North America. In New York he'd managed an Irish pub for a year and had hired several of his compatriots studying there as waiters and barstaff. 'I told each and every one of them they should not be rude to the Yanks in their own country, but they never listened to me,' he said. 'None of them did.' I wondered what Paddy meant by rude and asked him.

'Well, you know the Yanks, the ones who are always saying they're Irish. They'd chat with my staff and say, "So, you're Irish, are you? So am I." And the lads would always return with the same bleedin' lines: "Ah, so you'd be Irish, would you? Now what county would you be from then?" Put some of them right off their drink. They knew the lads were taking the piss. We lost business.' He shook his head. I wasn't going to tell him about Plastic Paddy – or his former president, Mrs Robinson, either.

A young woman on crutches asked us if the third stool at our table was free. I smiled and nodded and she sat down with some difficulty. Siobhán told us she was from Inis Oírr (Inisheer), the smallest of the three Aran Islands and a Fíor-Ghaeltacht too, although it lies just eight kilometres off the coast from Clare, a county firmly in the Galltacht but one that can boast some of the best traditional music in the country. Siobhán and Paddy exchanged a few sentences *as Gaeilge*, and then switched back to English. I couldn't tell whether they were doing it for my sake out of politeness or whether there was some tacit agreement between native speakers and secondary learners that, having communicated in the 'first official language', the 'other' one was their lingua franca.

I asked Siobhán whether she thought attitudes towards Irish had changed much since she was a child. 'Well, ya know, when we were kids, we used to whisper to one another in Irish when we'd come to a place like Galway,' she said. 'It was a bit embarrassing speaking it, ya know? But now look at this.' She gestured toward Paddy and then to me. 'Everything about the language has changed.

Paddy snorted and shook his head. 'Irish has become posh,' he said dismissively. 'It's all a middle-class phenomenon. The working class isn't participating in this linguistic renaissance – or whatever they want to call it – at all. But I do know one thing: if Irish hadn't been made the official language of the country, it would be doing a lot better than it is now. Like Welsh is.'

Siobhán was staring at Paddy without saying a word. I'd heard the debate over whether or not statehood had helped Irish very much over the last eight decades but wanted to know what she thought of Paddy's assessment. 'He's got a point,' she said. 'Forcing something on someone doesn't gain you much love or respect. And the way it was taught in school! Sometimes I wonder whether the teachers even liked it. For kids outside the Gaeltacht it was like learning Latin, something that was hard and boring because it was taught that way. A kind of torture. Something they knew they'd never use once they left school or got a place in university.'

Did people in the Gaeltacht know how outsiders felt about their language? 'Of course we did,' she said. 'How could we not?

We'd hear them sniggering and calling us "the Irish over there". As if they weren't. It hurt, yes.'

And now everything had changed? 'It's really not fair of me to say,' she laughed. 'I've been out of school for awhile now. You wouldn't know it though, would you? Kicking a football around with my little brother and spraining my ankle. Daft, really.'

The Galway Gaeltacht is the largest and most populous Irish-speaking district in Ireland; in some areas of Connemara, more than 90 per cent of adults speak Irish every day. It is also the most vibrant. The Gaeltacht Civil Rights Movement was born here in the late 1960s, which led to the establishment of the country's first Irish-only radio station, Raidió na Gaeltachta (Gaeltacht Radio), which still broadcasts from Casla (Costelloe). The studios of TG4, the popular Irish-language television station, are nearby at Baile na hAbhann (Ballynahown) and the republic's only Irish-language newspaper, a weekly called *Foinse* (*Source*), is published here.

Of course I knew all about how self-confident and active this Gaeltacht was in keeping Irish alive as a community language. We were staying at An Cheathrú Rua – its epicentre judging from the number of phone calls placed to Raidió na Gaeltachta request-ing songs or voicing an opinion on talkback shows – and could see and hear that every day. I'd travelled beyond this base, to the Islands District with Seán and to little settlements with names like Ros Muc (Rosmuck) and Cill Chiaráin (Kilkieran), but I wanted to go farther afield this time around.

Despite the massive amounts of road construction that appeared to be tearing the country apart (in every sense) and could turn any journey into a game of wait and see, it was good to be back on the road again. In fact, I had almost missed driving when I took that break in Galway to get my fix of pasta and con-crete beneath my feet.

I liked the way Irish motorists drove, and the etiquette of the road in rural Ireland. Irish drivers almost always seemed to signal some sort of greeting as they passed one another along country roads. It might be a flick, a nod or a twitch of the head, or an index finger extended upward from the top of the steering wheel. Sometimes they'd point at me, making me fear at first that I was doing something wrong, that my lights were on or my wheel was wobbling. Before long I learned that it was just an acknowledgement of a shared experience, as close as two motorists passing one another on an open road could get to interacting. I started doing it too.

The Great Blasket stayed lodged in my mind as I travelled west from Galway and through Cois Fharraige, the 35-kilometre coastal strip called 'Seaside' in Irish and the same road we'd followed when we first entered Connemara all those weeks before. I drove into An Spidéal (Spiddal), past the huge crafts centre called An Ceardlann (The Workshop), which must have been the largest Irish-speaking 'mall' in the country, and An Crúiscín Lán, a pub optimistically called 'The Full Jug' where we'd all gone to hear Johnny Connolly play the melodeon after being starved of traditional music in An Cheathrú Rua. Without giving it much thought, I turned south short of Costelloe and found myself approaching the ferry pier at Rossaveal. I was island-bound again, heading for Inis Mór (Inishmore), the largest of the three Aran Islands and the one I'd spent so much time staring at from the Beach in the Middle. '*Tá croí na Gaeltachta sna n-oileán fós* (The heart of the Gaeltacht remains in the islands),' an old man in An Cheathrú Rua had told me. I hoped I was on the right track.

The boat left almost immediately, the gulls in noisy pursuit as we slipped out of Cashla Bay, past the graveyard and the roofless church with its eternal flame inside. The sea was as calm as I'd seen it since I'd arrived in Ireland, and the Italian and Spanish tourists sitting on the benches along the side of the boat relaxed, resting their feet on the guardrails and tilting their faces back in an attempt to catch what little sun the Irish coast could offer on a late summer's morning. With a little luck and fewer clouds in the sky, they might return at least a shade darker.

A scrum of students on a school trip from a Dublin *Gaelscoil* (Irish-language school) crowded the bow. They were disappointed that their slickers and trainers were still dry and would apparently remain that way for the length of the journey. They horsed around and tried to rock the boat, but it would take more than a bit of jumping and spinning to have any effect on the colossal *Aran Flyer*. The students had expected a more dramatic crossing than this, and when I told them about the trips to Inishmaan and the Great Blasket, the boys whistled in delight and all but congratulated me for having survived such life-threatening experiences. Admittedly I'd added the parts about the lifeboats being lowered, but they'd asked me '*Cén scéal?*' when we first met and I wasn't about to disappoint them.

Inishmore is a relatively large island, measuring almost fifteen kilometres east to west, and I'd left my bike in Galway; I needed transport. The teenagers manning the fleet of rental bicycles at the end of the pier were chatting together in Irish, and when I asked the older one to lower the seat of the bike I'd chosen, he did so with a smile. My quest for the Gaelic grail in Inishmore looked promising.

I pedalled through Cill Rónáin (Kilronan), the main settlement, dodging the droves of visitors who had spent the night on the island or had arrived on the earlier boat from Rossaveal. Many of them were wearing new, oatmeal-coloured, 'hand-knit' jumpers, and they walked around aimlessly. Having done the IR£5 tour of the island in one of the dozens of white vans that now clogged the island's once empty roads and made all their purchases, there was nothing much left to do but wait for the ferry back to the mainland. High season was still roosting on Inishmore.

The road up to Dún Aonghasa (Dún Aengus) an enormous stone fort on the southern coast of the island, was quite steep and when I coaxed the bicycle a tad too forcefully the chain jammed and refused to submit to any pulling; I had to drag it up the hill. A woman running the souvenir shop at the foot of the path leading up to the fort had dealt with these problems before and knew the solutions to all of them. She told me I'd find a replacement bike behind the stone wall and to leave the immobilised one in its place. Somebody would eventually come to take it away and try to make it right, she assured me.

Legend had it that the fort was built by Aonghas, the leader of an early Celtic tribe that had found its way this far west. The fort was as old as the *cashel* on Inishmaan – Aonghas' brother Conchubhar built that one – but was much larger. It also had an infinitely more dramatic location, perched on a sheer cliff and facing west, with Newfoundland the next landfall. The drop must have been almost 100 metres into a sea so furious at being restrained that it had battered great chunks out of the limestone walls.

I felt both exhilarated and frightened as I inched towards the edge of the cliff to peer down, and when I kicked a few pebbles over the side to see what effect they'd have on the foaming lunatic below, a guard appeared out of nowhere and raced towards me. 'You could kill yourself doing that, you ijit!' she shouted and led me away from the edge. It wouldn't have been the first time. Apparently a couple of years before a photographer visiting Inishmore had gone missing and a search was made but proved futile. It was only when a group of Japanese tourists saw an arm pointing out towards the horizon from a ledge near the surface of the water that the truth was known.

With the fear of God and steep drop-offs firmly re-registered, I carried on westward, stopping to chat with an old farmer who was raking hay in a tiny field next to the ruins of a group of ancient churches and to watch – along with tourists in another one of those little white vans – seals cavort in the waters of a small bay on the north coast. When I returned to Kilronan late in the afternoon, I stopped in at the American Bar, despite (or perhaps because of) its name, a place that I'd heard was popular with local people.

I asked the young woman behind the bar for *pionta Guinness* and she looked at me blankly. 'Sorry, I don't have any Irish,' she said. 'What will you be having in English?' She was a South African on a working holiday and hadn't got to the 'pint' stage yet. 'None of the local people want to do this kind of work in sea-

son,' she said. 'They all go into hiding. Come back in winter.
You'll hear plenty of Irish then, I expect.'

Summer was still with me, though late in the season, and winter
more a distant memory than a coming reality. Heading north, I
decided to give most of what remained of the Mayo Gaeltacht a
wide berth; the area where I could expect to find a real concen-
tration of Irish speakers was in Ceathrú Thaidgh (Carrowteige), a
small, isolated pocket of perhaps 300 people on the coast in the
far north-west of the county. Instead, I drove up through the barren, mountainous region called Joyce County and then down to
the shores of Lough Corrib, a large but shallow lake studded with
islets, one of which was where the sixteenth-century pirate and
Queen of Connacht, Gráinne Uí Máille, known to the world as
Grace O'Malley, once made her home.

I drove through Corr na Móna (Cornamona), an attractive little settlement ringed by mountains that gazes down a narrow finger of land thrust into the lake. A sign pointed down a small lane
to Áras Bhríde. Was it a 'Maiden's Centre' or 'Bridey's'? Once,
in An Cheathrú Rua, Bridey had told me how much she loved
Cornamona and would love to live there. 'Oh, but the winds!'
she'd said. 'In winter they whip down those mountains to the
lake, and it's so bitterly cold.' Would she miss the sea, the stones,
the Irish words for 'No Verges' and 'Loose Chippings' on the
signs that she passed along the road? Would the *craic* be less fun
here than in An Cheathrú Rua? Would the publican look at her
blankly and deny any knowledge of *an Ghaeilge* should she ask
'Pionta Guinness, más é do thoil é?'

The road zigzagged out of County Galway into Mayo and I
could hear Alice repeating 'County Mayo, God save us!' like a
mantra and giggling. I couldn't see any need for salvation; the
road hugged the western shore of Lough Mask, smaller and less
dramatic than Corrib but a lake nonetheless, full of hidden coves
and birdlife. This was another Irish-speaking area, but because it

is so far removed from the Mayo Gaeltacht to the north-west, it is usually lumped together with the Galway one. Perhaps that isn't the only reason though.

When I arrived in Tuar Mhic Éadaigh (Tourmakeady), a hard-scrabble village wedged between the lake and the Partry Mountains, with a sprinkling of houses, a lakeside pub and the remains of what looked like an old cinema, I stopped at the post office. The woman at the counter sorted the handful of postcards I'd hastily scribbled in the darkened corners of pubs and on bedside tables, doing the sums aloud in an Irish that would have been used in An Cheathrú Rua. It sounded familiar and would have drawn me back to Connemara had I not set my sights on the large Gaeltacht to the north where the dialect still sounded almost as unfamiliar to me as when I first heard Irish.

The village of Gleann Cholm Cille (Glencolumbkille) in Donegal lies in a Breac-Ghaeltacht, with only about a third of the adults still speaking Irish regularly. But it is the site of Oideas Gael at the Foras Cultúir Uladh (Ulster Cultural Institute), a centre that attracts even more foreigners wanting to study Irish language and culture than the Áras Uí Chadhain in Connemara. I was anxious to have a look and meet the language activist behind this association called 'Irish Instruction', so I resisted the magnet pulling me even farther north and headed west from Donegal Town and odoriferous Killybegs, Ireland's most important fishing port, which looked like it was being rebuilt from the bottom up.

Glencolumbkille's physical setting is certainly a major draw. The village of some 260 people lies at the end of a wide and mountainous peninsula, overlooking a bay fringed with white sand. There are other beaches and excellent walking in the Blue Stack Mountains too, and at the Folk Village Museum, set up by a community leader and priest in the 1960s, you can taste things like wine made from seaweed.

Liam Ó Cuinneagáin showed me around the centre, where students conjugate irregular verbs, learn to play the *bodhrán* and flute and throw pots. He was from 'the Glen' and held the first Irish-language course here in 1984. Some 120 people had attended the summer course that had just ended, half of them from outside Ireland. Liam remained passionate not just about teaching the language to outsiders but also about preserving it as a community language in the district.

'There's a healthier attitude towards the language nowadays, for sure,' he told me. 'Glen was a planted community from the seventeenth century and English has been spoken in the village for centuries. When I was a boy, I'd hear people from the country telling one another to "be looking for the English" as they approached town.' Once a Glen man they called 'the Horse' returned from working in Britain and spoke to them in English. 'Oh, I threw the Irish over my shoulder once I boarded the boat at Dun Laoghaire,' he explained. When Liam and other children in the area were sent to a boarding school in Letterkenny to do the School Leaving Certificate, they were teased as the 'fais, fats and fears' because they couldn't pronounce the 'w' in why, what and where.

'But this positive attitude hasn't filtered down to the family,' said Liam. 'The young speak Irish and then cast it off for English. They don't make the choice of Irish *and* English. Just go listen to children in the playground at school. That's the true test.'

And the future? 'Irish may be working as a network language,' he said, 'but it's under threat as a community language and it may be too late for the media, including television, to keep it alive as one. It will never die but will change form and status, spoken perhaps in certain art, literary or *sean-nós* circles.'

To someone attuned to hearing Irish as it is spoken in Connemara, Ulster Irish at first sounds incomprehensible, with all those 'j' and 'ch' sounds where there should be 'd' and 't' ones and the 'oo' sound at the end of so many words. On my way to Glencolumbkille I'd stopped in Teileann (Teelin), a tiny fishing village on the southern coast of the peninsula where 40 per cent of the people speak Irish. When I asked a shop assistant the time, she pronounced the numbers and used a word for 'past' I'd never heard before. I wasn't encouraged by that. I'd just have to listen more carefully to the news and local interviews on Raidió na Gaeltachta as I drove, lowering the volume on some of the music they chose to play. Many traditional Irish songs sounded so chaotic, so undisciplined to me, with all the instruments going at once. Racial memory had obviously overlooked music, at least in my case.

Donegal has never been as militant as, say, Connemara in regards to the Irish language. There are several reasons for this. The country has traditionally had closer links with Belfast, which is in the same province of Ulster, and Scotland than the other Gaeltachts; the movement there has always been horizontal rather than vertical. In Donegal, Irish is the 'language of the heart', a private or domestic language, one that is okay for insiders but not outsiders to speak. Also, there were Irish colleges in Mayo, Connemara and Cork but not in Donegal, so Ulster Irish was all but overlooked during the standardisation of the language in the 1940s and 1950s. It had to adapt to the others where it could.

Like Connemara and Kerry, Donegal has its own Fíor-Ghaeltacht. It runs along the north-west coast and inland to Gaoth Dobhair (Gweedore) and Dún Lúiche (Dunlewy), the gateway to Glenveagh National Park. The main settlements on the coast, An Bun Beag (Bunbeg) and Doirí Beaga (Derrybeg), run together to form one long strip of restaurants, petrol stations, pubs and B&Bs catering to summer visitors. It's easy to leave this blight by following the signs marked *Trá* – the small English translation 'Beach' blotted out on a few of them – down the little lanes running to the west.

Along the way to Gweedore, I saw a sign announcing 'Tabhairne Leo/Leo's Pub: Home of Enya and Clannad' about a kilometre out of Croithlí (Crolly). Both Enya and Clannad sang in Irish sometimes; I was sure to meet some *Gaeilgeoirí* there. After I'd installed myself at a B&B called Teach hAnraoí, the French-sounding Irish for 'Henry's House', and surrendered all the 'who's' and 'what's' and 'why's' coaxed out of me by the friendly Irish-speaking owners, the little French restaurant down the road in Bunbeg sounded about right. But they'd run out of just about everything, even at that relatively early hour, and I had to settle for the Irish staple of *iasc agus sceallóga* (fish and chips). Leo's was next on the agenda.

The pub was a veritable shrine to Leo's daughter, Eithne Ní Bhraonáin – better known to the world as Enya – and her sisters, brothers and uncles who made up the group Clannad. Gold and platinum records lined the walls and a selection of their music was at the ready. And like every sacred spot worth its icons, relics and sombre lighting, it had its pilgrims too.

'Are there going to be famous people here tonight?' a young American asked the barman.

'I'd be surprised at that,' he answered. 'The Clannad people only show up from time to time, and Enya seldom comes over from Dublin. Maybe only at Christmas.' The American looked like he was going to burst into tears. Christmas was a very long way off. He turned to me and introduced himself. 'What brings you here?' asked Scott from Arizona. 'Were you expecting to see Enya too?'

I didn't admit that I was but told him about the course. He seemed puzzled. 'Where do they speak Irish?' he asked me. I told him that the staff almost certainly spoke it and addressed the barman: '*Dia duit. Cén chaoi a bhfuil tú? Pionta Guinness, le do thoil* (Hello. How are you? A pint of Guinness, please)'. Scott looked pleased with my efforts and so did the barman. In fact, he was so pleased he was laughing. 'We've got a Connemara man among us,' he said to his colleague, a woman fiddling with a mobile phone. 'We wouldn't be understanding the likes of you,' he teased me.

'Come on, don't you ever watch "Ros na Rún" on TG4?' I countered. 'You'll hear lots of Connemara Irish on that.'

'And not understand it,' said the Mobile Maiden. 'There are a couple of characters from Donegal though. I can't bear to listen to that slag what's-her-name. She sounds like she just walked off a Gaoth Dobhair bog. It's horrible to hear.'

Two more Americans arrived – this place was definitely on the trail – and we made the usual travellers' exchanges: where we'd been, where we were going, which pubs to check out, which B&Bs not to check into. They were members of a pipe band in Scranton, Pennsylvania, and of course were Irish somewhere down the line. That made Scott the odd man out in the group at the bar. He was a little bit of everything, he said, everything but Irish. 'You must be the first non-Irish Yank ever to walk into this pub,' said the barman. 'Everyone who comes here is Irish, or at least claims to be. If it weren't for you lot . . .'

He wasn't able to finish; Scott was concerned about how the evening was going to unfold. 'Will there be *any* music tonight?' he asked. He hadn't travelled all the way to the Home of Enya and Clannad to hear talk about Irish-language television, Scranton, PA, and genealogies. He was going to persist, to make it happen.

'Oh, I should say so,' said the barman with a slight smirk on his face. 'I expect himself will be playing. There'll be no stopping him.' I took 'himself' to be Leo and wasn't at all surprised when an hour or so later an elderly man shouldering an accordion walked onto the small raised area in the back.

By that time the pub had begun to fill up with people. They were mostly an older crowd, disgorged from minibuses that had brought them down from the B&Bs lining the Bunbeg–Derrybeg road but a few strays took up their positions by the bar too. A Japanese couple with backpacks standing next to me nursed half-pints of Guinness, popping TicTacs into their mouths after each sip of the bitter brew.

Leo beamed at his audience and opened the set with a rollicking rendition of the reel 'The Swallow's Tail'. He finished by running his thumbnail along the length of the keyboard, and the audience applauded enthusiastically. Encouraged, he launched into a series of tunes familiar to anyone who's ever attended an Irish wedding anywhere. Almost everyone in the pub had; they were all moving their lips and tapping their feet. They didn't look like locals and they weren't Americans, but they did look different. I'd seen a fair few UK registration tags on the roads in this area and it had just dawned on me that that included Northern Ireland.

Ulster people visiting the other half of their province. And why not? This wasn't like West and East Germans in the old days. There wasn't any Wall.

I was steeling myself for 'Danny Boy' or the like and plotting my escape when I heard a voice whispering from behind me. 'He's pretty good, huh?' I turned to Scott, but he was chatting with the Japanese couple now that they'd given the Guinness and the TicTacs a rest, and the pipers had already crossed the road to their B&B to sleep off a day of hard driving and the half-dozen pints they'd sunk in record time. It was Alice, behind the bar and helping herself to a half-pint of lager. She saw me glance at it suspiciously and she shook her head. 'Don't worry, Ste. They won't be able to see that it's gone.'

That sounded about right. 'Actually, I was just about to go,' I said. 'I've had enough.'

'By which you mean the Guinness or the music?' asked Alice. 'You can never get enough of the first, I know that, but you like the music just as much as I do. You just won't admit it. It's too much like home, that's all. You're scared of that.'

Home? What the hell was this old woman . . . well, maybe not so old – our ages had converged by now. What was this woman talking about? 'Alice, I've got a long drive ahead of me tomorrow morning through County Tyrone down to the east coast,' I said. 'I want to go back to the B&B now.'

'Well, I'm having a fine time here at the moment, which is more than I can say I've had with you for awhile now, mister,' she said. 'I intend on staying and listening to some more music.' I ignored that threat. I knew she wouldn't – couldn't – hang about on her own. It just wouldn't work. 'And don't expect to hear from me tomorrow,' she added crossly. 'I don't like to go where the English are.'

I couldn't believe how silly she was being. I'd assumed all that had been forgotten long ago, what with the comedians on television and my having taken up residence in London and all. 'For Christ's sake, Alice, it's still Ireland. Don't you know anything? Most of the people in this room are probably over from Derry.' I pointed to the audience, beaming as they listened to Leo ham it up. 'What the hell difference could it make to you now anyway?'

Alice glowered at me; she didn't like me cursing. 'As I've always told you, there are three things you can't trust: a dog's mouth, a baby's bottom and the laughter of an Englishman,' she said, nodding her head smugly.

'All right, how about if we detour through County Down? We can keep an eye out for that black sheep of old you liked to sing about?' She knew I was teasing her and was none too pleased. 'Then meet me in Meath.' I started to laugh after managing that mouthful but her scowl remained firmly in place. It was no use talking sense to her at this stage. I glanced back at the bar as I stepped out the door. She'd gone of course.

Everything made me angry the next day as I drove north to explore the rest of the Donegal Gaeltacht: the roadworks, the monotonous sea moving in and out just as it had done the day before and the day before that, even the names of places. 'Bloody Foreland'. I said it over and over again. 'Bloody Foreland. Damn you, Alice, *damnú ort* and all your crazy, old-fashioned ways, your mixed-up ideas. *Go hIfreann leat* (To hell with you)! I'm in control here. These are my thoughts, my decisions. You're just along for the ride, a seagull perching on the back of the boat. Don't tread on the tail of me coat, Alice. Not now.'

Oileán Thoraigh (Tory Island) sounded like another curse, and from the pier at Machaire Uí Robhartaigh (Magheroarty), it appeared to be under siege – a barren, treeless speck of land pummelled by the wind and the waves. The island was still getting help in its battle though; about as many Irish-speaking people lived here as on the Great Blasket at the height of its glory, and fears of depopulation in the not-so-distant past had come to nothing. I contented myself with watching the island from afar. Even if I'd wanted to put out to sea again, to be agitated like a pellet in a spray can, there was no way to go. I'd missed the morning boat.

A desolate stretch of road led me through the shadow of Mount Errigal, a white-faced cone rising out of nowhere, through the Derryveagh Mountains and then south to the highway that cut through Letterkenny and the wounded market town of Omagh. Alice kept to her word, even after I'd crossed back over the border into County Monaghan and was in the republic again. I couldn't say for sure but I thought she might have heard my diatribe that morning. In any case, she stayed away as she'd said she would.

The Meath Gaeltacht is unique in Ireland. It is not a bastion of Irish speakers who have clung tenaciously to their language in the land of their ancestors but a planted community of *Gaeilgeoirí* brought here from impoverished and congested Gaeltachts in the mid-1930s on the promise of land, a house, basic livestock and a school for their children. The families who settled around Baile Ghib (Gibstown) came from a half-dozen different Irish-speaking areas in Connemara, Mayo and Kerry and spoke different dialects. English soon became the common language and that area remains a Gaeltacht in name only today.

The 300 or so people who settled at Ráth Cairn (Rathcairn) to the south-west all came from south Connemara, and it was a relatively successful mix from the start, despite the fact that Galltacht towns like Trim and Athboy are so close and Dublin is a mere fifty kilometres to the south-east. Today Rathcairn is a small but active Gaeltacht into its fourth generation, with a well-established Irish-language college and a community centre hosting cultural events.

The area around Rathcairn is lush but generally flat, with low-rising hills set off in the distance. I remembered how Seán had told us one night in An Cheathrú Rua about the two families he'd heard of as a boy from the Islands District who had agreed to relocate to Meath. They didn't want to go east but were excited about gaining ten hectares or so of land – a veritable estate by Connemara standards at the time – but when they awoke the first morning and looked around, they were disheartened. I could imagine how they must have felt. They'd exchanged the mountains and sea of Connemara for the lowlands of Meath and a tributary of the River Boyne.

I all but raced through Rathcairn – not difficult in such a small place – past the Coláiste Pobal Nua Ráth Cairn, an ultra-modern community college with a skylight running the length of one wing, a small shop with the innovative name of Siopa an Bhaile, or Town Shop, an ugly new church and a cultural centre called An Bradán Feasa, or The Salmon of Knowledge. That made me remember a story a teacher had told me in An Cheathrú Rua.

The Salmon of Knowledge was the name of the magical fish that the hero Fionn Mac Cumhaill inadvertently tasted, bestowing on him *fios gach feasa*, or the 'knowledge of all knowledge': wisdom, prophesy and the power of healing. The teacher had said that *eo*, an old Irish word for salmon, was the base of the word for knowledge: *eolas*. I'd finally learned why Alice had urged me to finish the fish on my plate on all those Fridays years before. 'It's good for ye brains, laddy,' she'd say in her funny Oirish accent. 'It'll polish up ye brains.'

The only signs of life now were the sheep worrying the grass in the field across the road from the centre. Rathcairn had closed for Sunday and it was probably just as well. It was time to start thinking about An Cheathrú Rua and home again.

Chapter IX

Irish Today, Irish Tomorrow

Where Irish is at the start of the third millennium and where the language is heading are questions that are frequently asked both in and outside Ireland. There are no simple answers, of course; it all depends who is doing the talking. Where Irish is now may be answered differently according to whether the respondent is sitting in a fish and chip shop in a Connemara Gaeltacht town, attending a Conradh na Gaeilge lecture series full of earnest language activists and fellow travellers, or standing in a queue at an all-but-monoglot English-language post office in Athlone. What the language's status and role will be in twenty years – much less a century – is anyone's guess.

The numbers game is a favourite of both proponents and detractors of the language. In the most recent census, taken in 1996, some 1.43 million people in the Republic of Ireland, or about 40 per cent of the total population, described themselves as being able to speak Irish. Almost a quarter of them said they spoke it every day. That would suggest that up to six times as many people use Irish on a daily basis outside the Gaeltacht as there are native speakers in the Irish-speaking districts themselves.

Statistics can distort or even lie, especially when an assessment, including the ability to speak a language, is made by the respondents themselves. Of the almost 354,000 people who told the census-takers that they spoke Irish daily, some 80 per cent were between the ages of three and nineteen. The number of so-called Irish speakers in the republic was clearly inflated by the large percentage of the population still at school, studying the language as a required subject and hearing it in some fashion every day. As far as these pupils and students were concerned, they were what the census returns would describe them as: daily speakers of Irish.

By way of contrast, of the total population of 1.6 million in Northern Ireland, where Irish is not a core curriculum subject in schools and has a lower status than Welsh does in Wales, for example, 79,000 people recorded themselves as being able to read, write and speak Irish in a census taken in 1991. Just over 142,000 said they were conversant in that language.

Competency levels in Irish peak between ages ten and fourteen in the republic and then fall dramatically; most of the adult population rarely or never use Irish. In the same 1996 census, for example, just over 39,000 people in the crucial age group of twenty to forty-four said they spoke the language daily. Most linguists in Ireland today put the number of 'real' daily speakers in the republic at about 71,000, or 2 per cent of the population, of whom almost a third live in the Gaeltacht.

As regards language ability, those whose knowledge of the language could be described as 'low passive', understanding less than half of what they hear or read, account for about 30 per cent of the population. Between 10 per cent and 14 per cent of those in the republic are 'competent' or 'more than passive' in Irish, understanding up to 80 per cent. Those who are actively competent in the language account for about 5 per cent of the population.

The distinctions between language ability, language use and language attitudes can get very blurred. While native speakers of Irish in the Gaeltacht have continued to abandon the language over the years in favour of English due to economic pressure, intermarriage or migration (internal and external), the number of people claiming to speak Irish nationally has increased faster than the population overall. Much of that has to do with changes in the way the language is now viewed.

What brought about the changes in attitude is difficult to pinpoint exactly – linguistics and sociologists will be debating that for generations – but the possible reasons are legion. Certainly prosperity – the new affluence resulting from the economic achievements of the so-called Celtic Tiger – brought a national self-confidence previously unknown to Ireland. Cultural successes abroad – from the surge of interest in Irish music, dance, literature and film to the formulaic but popular 'Irish' pubs that can be found everywhere from Boston to Budapest – brought Ireland to the attention of not just those in the diaspora but the world.

Further integration in the European Union has played a role. Again and again Irish people I encountered along the way told me that closer ties with Europe had them questioning what made them distinct from other Europeans. One of the answers, of course, was their ancient and unique language. If Catalan could not just exist but thrive in Spain alongside infinitely more widespread Spanish, why couldn't Irish do the same in predominantly English-speaking Ireland? On the other side of the English Channel a nation of 10 million people called themselves Belgians though 60 per cent spoke Flemish and 40 per cent French. Could Ireland follow the same route to which the government had been paying at least lip service since independence? How was it that Welsh had gone through such a renaissance?

This search for singularity may have been the natural result of disparate nations or groups forming a heterogeneous union as happened in the USA in the early twentieth century. Perhaps it was just the new luxury of a wealthier society being able to respond to appeals based on abstractions like culture, heritage and tradition. Interest in such things usually follows economic growth. In any case, Irish was no longer being looked upon as the language of the dispossessed or the uncouth tongue of peasants but as a cultural asset, something that set the Irish apart from their European cousins.

Other factors that helped to bring Irish to the fore and raise its status among much of the population run the gamut from the extensive work done by community organisations at the grassroots level both in and outside the Gaeltacht, and the increased use of the language among certain cultural organisations and businesses, to the surge of interest in the language in Northern Ireland. Arguably the most influential, however, have been the changes that have occurred in education and in the media in recent years.

In the past three decades, the growth in the number of *Gaelscoileanna*, government-assisted schools in which *all* subjects are taught in Irish, has been phenomenal. In the early 1970s, when a national voluntary organisation was set up to assist such schools, there were eleven primary and eight secondary *Gaelscoileanna* outside the Gaeltacht. At the start of the new millennium the number of Irish-medium primary schools had jumped to 134, and there were thirty-one secondary schools. The total number of pupils and students attending *Gaelscoileanna* was almost 26,000, or just under 4 per cent of the total enrolment at ordinary national schools at the primary and secondary levels. There is even talk of establishing university centres of education in the Gaeltacht.

In Northern Ireland there are fourteen primary schools and a secondary school in both Belfast and Derry that teach in Irish, some of which receive financial assistance from the British government. According to surveys, as much as 23 per cent of the Protestant community would support the teaching of Irish in schools.

The reasons for this vogue in Irish-language education are as numerous and varied as those for the general shift in attitude towards the language. Nationalism, patriotism, the desire to see their children educated in their ancestral language may be the motivations for some parents, but most who send their kids to *Gaelscoileanna* do so because they believe the standard of education to be higher than at the ordinary English-language national schools. The schools themselves are generally parent-driven and dynamic. The teachers are usually young and enthusiastic, the student body very active. Most important, the classes are much smaller than those in English-language schools, usually with only ten to twelve students.

Some parents argue in favour of the schools as social levellers. Schools continue to sprout up and enrolments to grow in working-class suburbs as fast as in middle-class areas; there are

Gaelscoileanna in North Dublin's run-down high-rise suburb of Ballymun and in Tallaght, a densely populated 'new town' to the south-west of the capital, as well as in the deprived South Hill district of Limerick.

Whether the Irish-medium schools will have any lasting impact on the development of the language remains to be seen. For a start, the momentum can't possibly continue as it has; the birth rate is declining in Ireland, as it is everywhere in Europe, and the numbers just won't be there soon. As it is now, many parents send their children to English-language secondary schools after they've completed their primary education at a *Gaelscoil*, possibly in the belief that *too* much Irish in favour of English may not be a good thing and that teaching materials and texts – always a problem in Irish-language schools – may not be up to scratch at a higher level. At the same time, though Irish-medium schools are assisted by state grants, the central government has sometimes been ambivalent about them, as they do not fall under its full control. The schools have also not enjoyed the full support of the Catholic Church as the clergy often sits on the boards of national schools and the *Gaelscoileanna* are mostly non-denominational.

In many ways even more influential in changing attitudes has been the country's first Irish-language television channel, which was launched under the less-than-inspired name of Teilifís na Gaeilge (Irish-language Television) in late 1996. Although the other two channels in the national system, Raidió Teilifís Éireann (RTÉ), particularly RTÉ 1, broadcast short programs in Irish, these are generally restricted to the odd cultural show in the morning, news headlines at lunchtime and the ten-minute *Nuacht* (News) bulletin in the late afternoon. With some cutting-edge programming, a widely watched soap opera set in a fictitious village in the Connemara Gaeltacht called 'Ros na Rún', and a couple of cult personalities like Hector the travel-show host and the soap-opera heart-throb Jason, what was later renamed TG4 brought the Irish language 'home' to more people than ever before. Even viewers who had previously denied having any knowledge – or memory – of the language were surprised to discover how much they could recall from their school days by following along with the subtitles.

There is no shortage of other Irish-language media for those who want or need it. Raidió na Gaeltachta (Gaeltacht Radio), based in Connemara, broadcasts throughout the country, though its content is generally very local and its selection of music rather conservative, at least according to younger listeners. A much hipper alternative is Raidió na Life (Liffey Radio), an independent Irish-language community station in Dublin that is on the air weekday evenings and throughout most of the day on weekends.

Magazines in Irish come and go – the most recent one to disappear was the relatively new journal *Cuisle* (*Pulse*) in mid-2000 – but there are two weekly newspapers. *Foinse* (*Source*) is a Sunday tabloid-format newspaper published in Connemara with a circulation of 8500 but, with all the colour and circus layout, it looks and feels more like a magazine. *Lá* (*Day*) is a more serious broadsheet published on Thursdays in Belfast. *Saol* (*Life*) is an official newsletter produced by a government body and distributed free each month. The *Irish Times* daily includes an Irish-language section a couple of times a week, including the popular *An Teanga Bheo* (*The Living Language*). Along with the press, more than 3000 Irish-language books are currently in print, with some 100 new titles published each year.

Ireland has a labyrinth of state agencies, bodies and commissions attached to various government departments that deal with Irish-language issues and policies – everything from the publication of school textbooks and new dictionaries to the accurate recording of place names in Irish and the language training of public-service personnel. The two most important, however, Foras na Gaeilge, formerly known as the Bord na Gaeilge, and Údarás na Gaeltachta, fall under the control of a ministry with a rather unwieldy name: the Department of Arts, Heritage, Gaeltacht and the Islands.

The department has been criticised for everything from its

muddled set of language policies to being directed by a minister who doesn't speak Irish. Several years ago, under pressure from Irish speakers, it promised to draft a Bille Teanga (Language Bill) to form the basis of a language act ensuring the community's linguistics rights under the constitution. The bill has yet to appear before parliament.

The government established the Bord na Gaeilge (Irish-language Board) in 1978 'to promote the Irish language as a vernacular of everyday communication', a task with which it has had varying degrees of success. It has now been supplanted by the Foras na Gaeilge (Irish-language Body), a cross-border executive with increased powers to promote the language in all thirty-two Irish counties. The message here, born out of the Good Friday Agreement of 1998, was that Irish was for everyone and should be accessible to all, in both the Republic of Ireland and in Northern Ireland.

The Foras na Gaeilge monitors implementation of the department's linguistic guidelines and, among other things, awards grants to Irish-language schools and publications like *Foinse* and *Lá* and distributes Irish-language books.

A large number of agencies deal with the infrastructure of the Gaeltacht, but the largest and most important governmental one is Údarás na Gaeltachta (Gaeltacht Authority) established in 1979. Although primarily the regional government agency responsible for the economic development of the Irish-speaking areas, it is also concerned with their social, cultural and linguistic growth. There has always been a catch-22 with that remit, however. Economic development of the Gaeltacht more often than not demands bringing in skilled outsiders – managers, technicians, tourism-industry staff, most of whom are monoglot English speakers – and that compromises the language. The criticism that the authority was not truly representative of the Gaeltacht was redressed in part in 1999 when the number of locally elected board members was increased to seventeen and the number of members appointed by the Gaeltacht ministry reduced to three.

Along with government bodies, dozens of non-governmental

and voluntary organisations are involved in endeavours to promote Irish at many different levels. They range from the long-established Conradh na Gaeilge (Gaelic League) and Comhdháil Náisiúnta na Gaeilge (National Irish Congress), an umbrella group of twenty-one member associations, to Gael-Linn, the first business-oriented Irish-language body set up in 1953. There is some overlap and exchange with state organisations and much of the financial assistance dispensed to them comes from National Lottery receipts.

While on my travels both in and out of the Gaeltacht, I was anxious to hear what people who had been working in or on behalf of Irish for much of their lives – linguists, historians, writers, journalists, government servants – had to say about the language today. Did they think that attitudes in general towards Irish had changed and if so, why? And, short of consulting crystal balls, what did they think the future had in store for it? This being Ireland I expected huge differences of opinion. I was prepared for anything.

In Galway I found my way back to the university, an elegant campus on the banks of the clear River Corrib and a place I thought I knew from previous visits. But I'd never ventured much farther beyond the refined Georgian quadrangle that greets visitors near the main entrance and the sloping, tree-lined lawns leading up to it. By the time I'd found my way through the tangle of modern concrete blocks and across a soulless concourse with placards announcing an upcoming meeting of the Cairde Sinn Féin (Friends of Sinn Féin), I was late for my appointment.

Louis de Paor, a handsome Irish-language poet with hair so red his head appeared to be ablaze, was waiting for me in the student coffee shop. Through the large plate-glass windows I could see the concourse filling up with students eagerly greeting one another with Continental-style pecks on the cheeks and handshakes. Louis and I had met briefly at a poetry reading he'd given at the language centre in An Cheathrú Rua, and he welcomed me like an old friend.

Louis told me he had grown up in Cork in an English-speaking household and had first learned Irish in school. 'Irish was the only subject taught with the same zeal as religion in the Ireland of the 1960s,' he said. 'It was all part of a great program of national renewal and was always the first lesson for two hours in the morning, when pupils were thought to be least resistant.' But unlike so many other students who hated Irish as a discipline and resisted it for eight years, Louis readily embraced the language.

'Irish was the most natural thing in the world to me,' he said. 'It made perfect sense and instantaneously made another world available.' I mentioned that old chestnut, racial memory, and he smiled. 'Irish did have an early and very deep resonance for me and when I started writing poetry, I found the literary traditions of Irish more useful than the English ones. The Irish lyrical poetry of the twentieth century was much closer to what I wanted to write.'

Like so many Irish both before and after him, Louis left Ireland to travel and ended up in Melbourne, where he lived for almost a decade and was awarded an Australian government writing grant. A grant to write in Irish in *Australia*? 'It was the beginning of multiculturalism there,' he said, and the new context was instrumental in changing the politics of language for him. 'Speaking Irish in the street was a political statement in Ireland at that time, whether we liked to admit it or not,' he said. 'That was not the case in Australia. Everyone there spoke one language or another. It all felt very natural.'

At home, Louis spoke Irish exclusively with his children but not with his wife. He lived in Oughterard, a town on the fringe of the Connemara Gaeltacht that he described as having a 'split mentality' towards Irish. If he wanted to conduct his business in Irish only, however, he knew what shops and other establishments to patronise. As an Irish speaker and writer, wouldn't it be better to live in the heart of the Gaeltacht instead of just on the fringe looking in?

Louis shook his head. 'It's not wise to go completely native,' he told me. 'There will always be a psychological distance between native speakers and those not born into the language. Native speakers of Irish have traditionally been resistant to learners and often answer back in English.' I'd heard and experienced that on several occasions along the way in the Gaeltacht but especially in Donegal, where Irish is said to be viewed by many as a lingua franca for the community and not a language for external use.

Did all that have something to do with self-protectionism? 'In a way, native speakers were made to feel custodians of traditional Irish culture and the Irish language,' he said. 'It was used to elevate them but at the same time could be used to abuse them.'

Still, both the real and the perceived borders separating the Gaeltacht from the English-speaking Galltacht were disappearing, he said. 'The perceived wisdom that bilingualism is impossible – that you have to choose one language or the other – is finished,' he told me. 'Everyone now accepts that you don't have to cease speaking Irish to speak English well.'

Louis cited many of the reasons I'd heard before for these shifts – Ireland's new affluence and increasing self-confidence, closer ties with Europe, the media – but he was quick to include the groundwork laid down by activists of the Gaeltacht Civil Rights Movement. 'The empowering of the community by the generations of the 1960s and 1970s cannot be underestimated,' he said.

I wondered whether speaking Irish had in fact become trendy, a badge of distinction, among certain young people. 'Irish is associated with the "new cool", but that may be transitory,' he said. 'At the very least, the cultural cringe is disappearing. I knew a girl in the Kerry Gaeltacht years ago who would get physically sick every time her parents sent her into Dingle to shop.' In fact, he said, 'in some quarters the cringe has gone the other way: that you are Irish and can't speak the language as well as you should'. He cited an interesting example. Louis' father, who spoke Irish as a learned language, preferred to use English with him and his brother because he believed he didn't speak it as well as his sons.

When I asked him about the future, Louis seemed guarded. 'People are giving up the language for whatever reason in the Gaeltacht,' he said. But apparently that wasn't the only problem: the structure of the language itself was under threat from English. 'It's okay for a language to borrow vocabulary and idioms from another – that's natural. But when it takes on new grammatical structures it loses its soul,' he said. 'The Irish in Connemara and Donegal follows English so closely at times that it is worrisome.'

'But will it collapse under the pressure and die?' I asked him, regretting immediately that I'd used the dreaded 'D' word.

'Languages don't die of natural causes,' he said. 'They are killed.'

The university's history department was not far away and I stopped in to chat with Dáibhí Ó Cróinín, a professor of early Irish history and the author of a surreal novel called *An Cúigiú Díochlaonadh* (*The Fifth Declension*) that I'd quickly realised was way over my head, both linguistically and intellectually. Perhaps I would have been better off sticking to something along the lines of the project he was working on at the time: a new Irish translation of *Pinocchio*.

Dáibhí told me that when the book was first published in Irish in 1933, *Pinocchio* was in a wonderfully idiomatic Irish and, of course, was directed at children. The new translation was being structured more along the lines of English and would serve as a university text. That sounded odd. 'You can't understand some Irish if you don't speak English nowadays,' he explained.

Almost everyone I spoke to told me they thought that Irish-language television was more crucial to the future of the language than any other medium. Not only had TG4 introduced Irish to the public in a more entertaining, natural way than ever before with its dramas, game shows and children's programs, it had also created jobs in Irish beyond teaching and the civil service. But Dáibhí seemed to disagree on its importance. 'It should have been done much earlier,' he said. 'It's all too much and too late now. We should have had it in the 1950s and 1960s.'

I wondered whether new writing in Irish would play a role and was surprised when, as a novelist himself, Dáibhí dismissed the idea. 'Nobody buys it and nobody reads it,' he said. 'If Irish-language literature were market-driven, it wouldn't exist.' That sounded a bit harsh and I said so. 'Let's just say about 300 people in the entire country read new literature in the Irish language. No more than that.'

Dáibhí told me he believed that while many people used to be actively opposed to speaking or answering questions in Irish in shops or on the street, they were now much more welcoming. 'Initially this new-found interest in the language started among those people who didn't have a syllable,' he said, freely admitting that the reasons why were not clear. 'Did they feel somehow cut off from the language? Was it a question of having a bad conscience?' I brought up the European Union. 'Perhaps the Irish want other Europeans to know that they can speak their own language,' he said. 'Or maybe they just don't want to be mistaken for being English.'

Dáibhí Ó Cróinín had sounded pessimistic about the Irish-speaking areas. 'Even the activists are despondent about the state of the language in the Gaeltacht,' he had told me. I walked over to the Áras na Gaeilge, the Irish-language centre on campus, to find out if that were true.

I had met Gearóid Denvir, an Irish teacher and self-proclaimed language activist, once before in Connemara, and he'd been full of opinions, peppering his speech with such colourful expressions as 'de Valera's wet dream' and the odd expletive. He was uncharacteristically subdued when I stopped by his office though. His wife had been away and he'd been put in charge of getting his young sons up, fed and off to school that morning. He looked exhausted.

'Though there is much more self-confidence in the Gaeltacht than in the past, the community must be aware that it is under enormous pressure,' said Gearóid. 'The rates of attrition are very high, with 75 per cent of Irish-speaking parents not raising their kids in the language.' But he saw a silver lining in this dark cloud: three times as many people in Dublin spoke Irish daily than in the Gaeltacht and twice as many in Cork, he said.

Gearóid disagreed that one had to speak English to understand some Irish today but acknowledged that the language had changed. 'It's only natural that there be an exchange between a minority language and a power one,' he said. 'The Irish of twenty-five years ago was of a higher standard for many reasons. Education everywhere is more child-motivated nowadays, and the three 'Rs' have broadened. The vocabulary range of younger Irish speakers is less great today, but older people have more time on their hands, more time for talk, so their vocabulary is greater.'

Would television help redress the problem? 'Television is over-exaggerated as an influence on language,' he said. 'The car has had a much greater impact as it brings mobility and outsiders into the areas – "white settlers" like Germans, Swedes, Americans and Britons and people marrying in who don't speak the language. This is what causes language shifts.'

I made a conscious effort to cleanse my mind of any 'colourful expressions' as I climbed the steps to the first floor of the Áras na Gaeilge. I was on my way to see Mícheál Mac Craith, a professor of modern Irish at the university who also happened to be a Franciscan priest. But he was both as erudite and down-to-earth as friends had described him and I probably could have got away with saying anything. When I asked him about changes in Irish over the past few decades, he used Irish-language television as an example.

'If you watch "Ros na Rún" on TG4, you'll hear that all the characters under twenty are bilingual and speak Irish accordingly,' he said. I wasn't sure I would be able to tell the difference, but I took Mícheál's word for it. 'The language gets progressively richer and more idiomatic until the sixty-plus bracket, when it is by far the richest,' he said. 'It's a diachronic thing. People over fifty tend to be more prescriptive when it comes to language. My father, for example, is constantly picking up "mistakes" when he reads Irish. Most of them are the grammatical and spelling changes made in the 1950s.'

I asked him about any shame his compatriots might feel for not being able to speak Irish today, and Mícheál mentioned the name of a poet who I knew by name only, having missed my chance to meet her in Dingle. 'Biddy Jenkins once remarked that it would be good if writers in the Irish language would go away so that English-language ones would not have to have bad consciences,' he said with a laugh.

I felt like I'd taken a flight to the moon and not just driven the length of the coastal road from Galway when I paid a visit to the headquarters of TG4 in Ballynahown. The state-of-the-art studios, in the shadow of a thirty-metre tall television tower, were housed in what looked like a space station next to the rocks and bogs of Connemara.

Cilian Fennell, TG4's programming director, poured me a cup of tea in the staff canteen as I watched the rain cascade on the barren landscape outside. I could hear a couple of young people outside in the corridor speaking excitedly in a mixture of English and Irish; staff there, whose average age was twenty-five, were a mix of native speakers and secondary learners.

With television's modern, relevant and even sexy image in general, and the impact the station had had on the language, I decided this was the place to determine once and for all whether Irish had become fashionable among young people.

'Irish was once associated with God and nationalism, Peig Sayers and Patrick Pearse,' Cilian told me. 'This is the first baggage-free generation to speak Irish. But cool?' Cilian looked doubtful. 'Let's just say it's always cool not to have baggage.'

The station's remit is to broadcast Irish-language programs for those who use or are learning the language and subtitle them for everyone else at certain times of the day. 'First came the spoken, then the written and now the visual,' said Cilian. 'But we are a television station – not a language movement or museum. We broadcast and empower the community, but television belongs to everyone and the station is open to all.' The station was always intended to be national and not regional. Thus its original name – Teilifís na Gaeilge – which refers to the Irish language, not the Irish-speaking districts.

TG4, which is a public company under the RTÉ umbrella, has created a lot of jobs locally and not just for the sixty full- and part-time staff working at the station itself. In the early 1990s, Údarás na Gaeltachta started television production classes for Irish speakers, a move that met with a fair amount of criticism in the days when Irish television didn't even exist. The courses spawned a number of small, independent production companies that now supply TG4, which produces little on its own, with the bulk of its programming. In fact, almost 80 per cent of the IR£14 million annual budget goes to them.

'The Irish-speaking community now has its own voice rather than one coming from the outside,' said Cilian, 'and the world is interested in this Irish insight on the world and how they view themselves.' On the television monitor behind him I could see the channel's motto: '*Súil Eile*', or 'Another Eye'. TG4 now has 85 per cent saturation in the republic and upwards of 600,000 viewers.

At the start of the new millennium TG4 was on the air nineteen hours a day in English and Irish, though seven hours were relayed Euronews broadcasts. Originally the station was to broadcast in Irish two hours a day. That amount has now been tripled, with three hours dedicated to children's programs and three for adults.

The channel has a mixed programming schedule. In Irish, there's news, sports, children's and game shows, travel programs, documentaries, soap operas and situation comedies, all of which are subtitled in English after 10 p.m. on weekdays and all day long on weekends for non-Irish speakers and learners. Some of the most popular programs have been 'Ros na Rún', a kind of 'Peyton Place' set in a country town with all the usual goings-on (divorce, adultery, homosexuality and so on), a comedy called 'CU Burn' about a pair of ambitious undertaker brothers who set up Ireland's first turf-fired crematorium, and another one called 'Gleann Ceo' in which two police officers with time on their hands invent crimes so that their *Garda* station in a quiet Donegal village won't be shut down.

'We don't do things in Irish just to please people,' Cilian told me, 'but stereotypes can be fun, so why not?' Non-Irish programs include old movies, top-forty music shows and Euronews. These are not subtitled as it is assumed that, while not all English speakers have Irish, Irish speakers always understand English. Commercials are almost always in English, except for a couple of memorable ones for KitKat and Guinness.

No particular dialect is favoured on TG4; there are weather announcers from Connemara and Kerry, a news anchorperson from Ulster and a sports announcer from Waterford. 'Of course everyone wants to hear their own accent,' said Cilian, 'and they can, but they have to get the gig.' In general this is not a problem as most broadcasters on TG4 blunt their accents for viewers. But occasionally the station has to use subtitles in Irish, when a farmer from north-west Donegal speaks in a particularly thick Ulster accent, say, or a new or seldom-used word such as *urghaire* (injunction) is used. A language movement or teaching agency it may not be, but even Irish speakers are still learning.

The studios of Raidió na Gaeltachta were not far away – just up the road, in fact, in Costelloe – but I knew I'd returned to earth when I pulled into the drive. The studios were older and more established than TG4's, running higgledy-piggledy across lawns that gained a foothold long ago in the harsh landscape. Raidió na Gaeltachta can trace its origins to a much more dramatic era: the heady days of the Gaeltacht Civil Rights Movement of the 1960s and 1970s, when a young generation of Irish speakers sought new focus for their language and traditional culture.

The first Irish-language radio station was a pirate one called Saor Raidió Chonamara (Free Connemara Radio) set up at Rosmuck in 1970; until then the only two choices in Ireland were Raidió Éireann, which broadcast almost exclusively in English, and Radio Luxembourg. The government established Raidió na Gaeltachta in 1972 after much agitation by the Civil Rights Movement, including a walkathon from Carna to Barna in protest against private ownership of lakes and rivers in the Gaeltacht.

The station was originally set up to serve the Gaeltacht with a couple of hours of news and other programs per day. Today it can be heard *ar fud na tíre*, 'throughout the country', as its logo states, some sixteen and a half hours a day, with plans to go to twenty-four hours by 2002 and to broadcast on the Internet. It has a listening audience of 106,000, two-thirds of whom live outside the Gaeltacht, and another 30,000 in Northern Ireland, and employs some seventy full- and part-time staff in Costelloe and four other studios in the Gaeltacht. Most of the staff are native speakers in their thirties.

Raidió na Gaeltachta, part of the RTÉ public broadcasting system with no advertising, is top-heavy with current affairs and magazine shows, local talkback programs, Irish music and sports. The most popular broadcasts are the lunchtime news, covering local items of interest to Irish speakers (in other words, the Gaeltacht areas in the west, north and south) for the first half-hour followed by national and international items for the next thirty minutes, and the local notices from four to six o'clock. There are also programs dealing with books and the Irish language, and a story hour. At times, Raidió na Gaeltachta sounds like a country radio station in rural America or Australia.

According to Seán O' hÉanaigh, director of programming at the station and a native speaker who returned to the area as a child from the USA with his emigrant parents, that is the key to its success. 'Raidió na Gaeltachta has not reacted to commercial forces,' he told me, 'and has stayed true to its remit.'

Seán credited the station with helping unite the various Irish dialects, a seemingly insurmountable task in the past and one that flummoxed even language planners. 'Nowadays, Irish-speaking people can understand one another with little or no problem,' he said, 'and hearing the different dialects is usual because of the radio station.' I'd heard that before.

'If it weren't for Raidió na Gaeltachta, it would still be the Dark Ages for dialects in Ireland,' Liam Ó Cuinneagáin of Oideas Gael had told me in Glencolumbkille.

The station was also instrumental in reviving certain forms of traditional music. '*Sean-nós* singing was dying until Raidió na Gaeltachta came along,' Seán told me. It's certainly very much alive today; the a cappella 'old-style' ballads can be heard throughout the day on the station. Raidió na Gaeltachta is aware that this may no longer be to everyone's tastes, particularly those of a new generation of listeners. It also broadcasts other types of music, including a popular program of world music.

'Irish has become cool in the last decade,' Seán said. 'It's almost a badge of distinction. People travel a lot nowadays and wonder why they can't have their own language like other Europeans.'

As I was preparing to leave, Seán introduced me to the station's director, Tomás Mac Con Iomaire, who stopped to chat. He asked me where I was from and when I told him, he began talking about Fields Corner and the area where my father grew up as if it were his home village. 'You'll be hearing a lot of Irish in the pubs on Dorchester Avenue on a Saturday night – maybe even more than in some parts of Connemara,' he said with a laugh.

Certainly I'd hear more Irish on 'Dot Ave' than in Dublin unless I sought it out, which was exactly what I intended to do when I headed for the capital. I was still transfixed by the concept of the Irish language being *faiseanta* – 'fashionable', 'stylish', 'à la mode', if you will – and imagined bouncers at trendy clubs like POD and Rí-Rá ordering aspiring entrants to the back of the queue *as Gaeilge* and well-dressed young salestaff with lilting Kerry accents helping me choose a woollen pullover.

I didn't see or hear much of that sort of thing after a day and night in pursuit of it. The bouncer was from North Dublin and the sales assistant, every bit as fashionable as I'd imagined, sounded more Essex than Éire; she'd grown up in Chelmsford. I decided to check out some of the 'Irish-only' restaurants-cum-coffee shops I'd heard about instead.

Dáil Bia, which combines the words for 'encounter' or 'meeting' with 'food', was below the Comhdháil Náisiúnta na Gaeilge (National Irish Congress) on Kildare Street (or Sráid Cill Dara as they most likely called it there), and I stopped by for a coffee one late summer morning. I probably could have used something stronger.

I'd been to a play the night before at a small playhouse called THEatre Space on Henry Place around the corner from the GPO. The play was a black comedy called *Paddy Irishman, Paddy Englishman and Paddy..?* about two Irish guys, Kevin and Anto, living in a shabby Kilburn bedsit in London who had to decide where their loyalties lay after one of them inadvertently got mixed up with the IRA. Alienation, nostalgia for the homeland, lots of drinking and a fight – that sounded as Irish as I'd find on stage in Dublin that evening. In the middle of their skirmish Kevin fell on a pint glass and split open his forehead. Not great acting and high-tech props – for real this time. The blood was spouting across the stage like Old Faithful itself and we were told to leave while 'Kevin' was hurried into an ambulance.

Later that evening my appetite had gone into hiding when I joined a friend for supper at a small bistro in Castlemarket. Feeling even more queasy when a somewhat underdone lamb chop found its way in front of me, I went upstairs to the toilet and passed a table of shabbily dressed men whispering conspiratorially in Irish. '*Dia duit,*' I said cheerfully as I walked by and four glowering, almost hostile faces turned towards me.

'Did you see those guys upstairs?' my companion asked me when I'd returned to the table and my bloody chop. 'They looked like mafiosi.' I didn't think mafiosi spoke Irish – not yet, anyway. They looked to me like characters from a play.

Now in Dáil Bia, I relaxed as I heard all the other patrons around me chatting cheerfully in Irish – it was like being in the fish and chip shop in An Cheathrú Rua again – and when I asked the waitress what was for lunch she rattled off the short menu *as*

Gaeilge. No deep-fried place this; I'd entered raspberry vinaigrette and precious pasta territory. It was odd to be in a modern city, sitting in a café just off a fashionable shopping street and hearing Irish used in a modern and fashionable way.

Another café I visited, Caife Trí D (Café Three-D) – a word play on its address at 3 Dawson Street – seemed to attract a younger crowd and the staff acted more comfortable speaking English with customers though they spoke Irish among themselves. 'You're sitting in the non-smoking section, I'm afraid,' a waiter told me when I lit a cigarette, and then graciously helped me move my cup of coffee and bags to a table in the front.

There was none of that at the Club Chonradh na Gaeilge (Gaelic League Club) on Harcourt Street. It always seemed to be empty, as did Siopa Leabhair, the rather sombre Irish-language bookshop above it. The only other browsers I encountered were a couple of young Japanese backpackers who had somehow found their way there. They looked both confused and bemused by the titles on the spines of the books and eventually bought a postcard.

The offices of Foras na Gaeilge were not far away, in a lovely ivy-covered Georgian terrace facing Merrion Square. I met with Éamonn Ó hArgáin, the person charged with overseeing the communications, community and business sectors. He'd been detained for an hour and a half some years before by incredulous officers at Birmingham airport in Britain – part of Europe and the EU when last heard from – because his documents were all in Irish. He was still talking about it.

'We don't want to see the language used just in pockets around the country,' he said. 'Our policy is to push for total bilingualism, especially at government levels.' That sounded ambitious. 'Well, they can start by ensuring that Irish is available at all state offices.'

But didn't government policy state that every citizen had the right to conduct business with the public service through Irish?

'It's policy on paper,' he said. 'Until now there has not been any real state support.' He said he always had problems dealing with state organisations when he tried to use Irish. 'You call for information and they'll tell you "Sorry, the guy with Irish is off sick today",' he said. 'The passport office is the only one fully in Irish. It's frustrating for Irish speakers.'

I wondered how private enterprises could be won over if even the public sector was dragging its feet. 'When the state supports these initiatives, business follows,' Éamonn said. To some degree they have. A number of retailers, including ones with a strong Irish brand such as the Eason chain of bookshops and Dunnes Stores, use Irish to a much greater extent than ever before. It's seen, for example, on the forecourt signage at all TOP petrol stations around the country. Was it just a drop in the bucket? 'Probably about 10 per cent of all businesses want to do business in Irish today,' he said. 'That's the best-case scenario at present.'

We spoke about the state of Irish in the North with the advent of Foras na Gaeilge. 'West Belfast could almost pass as a Breac-Ghaeltacht,' said Éamonn, referring to the mixed English and Irish-speaking communities found in the republic. Apparently there was even an Irish-speaking café called Caife Glas (Green Café) near the Fallswater Road. Of course, there are more than just the obvious differences on both sides of the borders, including linguistic ones. The body had recently launched a campaign to promote the increased use of Irish with the slogan '*Scaoil amach é!*', a perfectly acceptable phrase meaning 'Let it out!' Unfortunately, north of the border it has the idiomatic meaning of 'Fire!' or 'Shoot!' '*Abair amach é*' or 'Say it aloud' was a more appropriate choice.

In 1990 Reg Hindley, a senior lecturer in geography at the University of Bradford in Britain and a socialist, published *The Death of the Irish Language: A Qualified Obituary*, the first work of its kind on Ireland. Based on field research and statistical analysis, the book concluded that Irish was indeed in its death throes and would disappear as a first language in a generation or two at most. Hindley set 10,000 as the upper limit of native speakers and suggested that Irish could not possibly survive full bilingualism. Who would use the minority language if everyone spoke the majority one? Much of the romantic appeal of the language would die with the Gaeltacht, he wrote, and Irish would become the property of scholars, priests and the 'linguistically long-anglicised bourgeoisie . . . in Dublin'.

The book caused an uproar in Ireland and sparked a national debate that continues to some extent today. Hindley was criticised for his methodology, out-of-date data, definitions and Marxist paradigm. Detractors questioned his exclusion of secondary learners from the total counts and his use of natural and biological metaphors like 'death', 'birth' and 'tide of history'. Many claimed he'd come to Ireland with an agenda.

The most widely read retort to the book was a pamphlet called 'Buried Alive: A Reply to The Death of the Irish Language' by Éamon Ó Ciosáin, a lecturer in French at the National University of Ireland at Maynooth. But both the book and the pamphlet had appeared at a time when, as Hindley put it, Ireland was 'one of the English-speaking world's economically weakest members', well before Irish-language television and the Good Friday Agreement that led to the creation of a cross-border body like Foras na Gaeilge. A lot had happened since then.

I caught the bus to Lucan, just west of Dublin, passing a sign that read 'Beál Feirsde 162 km' along the way. Wasn't 'Belfast' spelled Beál Feirste in Irish? Louis de Paor had told me that he reckoned up to half of the Irish-language road signs in Ireland had mistakes on them.

Éamon Ó Ciosáin was waiting for me at the Spa Hotel, a big old pile of a landmark on the N4 motorway, and we walked over to his house.

In the kitchen his two young daughters were playing while speaking in a mixture of Irish and English. 'What plastic tree?' I heard one shout to the other and tried to work out the question in Irish. I didn't have plastic. Would they accept a *rubar* tree?

One of the things that had angered Éamon most about *The Death of the Irish Language*, he told me, was its role in the refusal by the British Department of Education and Science to include Irish in a list of minority languages to be taught in UK schools. It wasn't until eight years later that Irish would become a recognised subject on the national curriculum in the United Kingdom.

'There was a bit of a turn in attitude towards Irish in the 1970s and a definite process of change in the 1980s,' Éamon said. He put it down to the confidence inspired by political movements in the Gaeltacht, the mushrooming of Irish-language nursery schools and what he called the 'linguistic economy'. It seemed that renewed interest in Irish had spawned a whole industry. 'People realised they could actually make a career out of Irish,' he said. 'That was a big change.'

What about Europe? 'The language situation in Ireland is not exceptional,' he said. 'Other places are in the same boat. But minority languages are the flavour of the month now. People here began thinking they too could have something of their own.'

Éamon seemed less optimistic about the state of Irish and the Gaeltacht, even mentioning An Cheathrú Rua, where he'd spent three months studying Irish as a teenager. 'The language is school-bound,' he said, 'and the standard of Irish is low. There is still no all-Irish dictionary or an atlas of the world in the language. Families in the Gaeltacht are switching to English every week and no efforts are being made to stop it.' Wasn't the financial assistance the government provided Irish-speaking families there helping? 'The *deontas* and the housing grant schemes have created a lot of resentment outside the Gaeltacht,' he said. 'It's looked upon as paying them to speak their own language.'

He mentioned TG4's influence young Irish-speakers, especially in the Gaeltacht. 'In fact, I heard that some people were so encouraged by it that they left the television on even while they were doing things like vacuuming to help boost the ratings.'

'Irish is not necessarily considered hip in the Gaeltacht,' he said, 'but in cities like Dublin, yes, it's cool to know Irish, to have an interest in it, to be Celtic. Just listen to Raidió na Life. There's a lot more confidence in things Irish.' That would make a change from the days when some of the people in his neighbourhood called the Irish-speaking family down the road 'the Irish'.

In general, Irish in the early twenty-first century is in relatively good shape and improved attitudes (or at least lowered resistance) towards it have opened the doors wider to the restoration of the language – if not to a fully bilingual society – than they have been since independence. But there are no simple answers; there never are.

A man standing next to me in pub in Temple Bar one night was annoyed that the people beside him were speaking in Irish; he considered speaking Irish in public outside the Gaeltacht to be posy, the property of extremists and fanatics, he told me. Had he been to the Gaeltacht? He had, he said, but was even more annoyed than he was now. Everyone around him there had been speaking English.

Chapter X

Home

Things quietened down in the final weeks of the course in An Cheathrú Rua, more or less returning to the way they'd been at the start. Much of the transition had to do with refocusing, I think. Though there was still plenty of time to add a string of new words or even another verb tense or noun declension to their repertoires, most of the students had reached as far as they were going to get, at least this time around, in their search for Irish. Had we all reached the goals we'd set for ourselves on the bus from Galway to An Cheathrú Rua? That was hard to say. Most of us probably didn't know the answer anyway.

Some people were getting ready for the main social event of the course – 'Oíche Mhór Cheoil'. The 'Big Music Night' was traditionally held at An Dóilín Hotel on the evening of the last day of class. It was a kind of talent show at which students were invited to perform a set piece of just about anything they chose – short of human sacrifice and anything else that went against the laws of the state and the Holy Catholic Church – before the teachers and staff of the Áras Uí Chadhain and the host families. They could be heard strumming on harps and guitars, practising intricate dance steps and learning yet another Irish folk song with verses that would go on into the next millennium. I thought for a moment that I'd been transported to the sound stage of *Fame*.

Those who had enrolled in the course for university credit were preparing for their final *scrúdú*. Although it was an oral test, this was an 'exam' after all and, with such a forbidding-sounding Irish name, preparations for it were being taken seriously. I'd seen students revising on the stone walls in front of the centre during the lunch break, reviewing while stretched out on the squeaky sands of Coral Beach in the late afternoon with their study sheets fluttering in the wind, and even cramming at the picnic tables outside An Chistin, fingering their little green dictionaries like talismans. There was no longer any time to look back on the past and wonder how things might have been; the present and the future were the forms to follow now. Everyone was busy.

We were all looking forward to a break on the last free Saturday afternoon, however, an escape from all this diligence and earnest activity. A boat race was to be held from the pier just north of Coral Beach on the Bay of the Great Man, with hookers and other sailing vessels competing for the top prize; someone had even opened a book on it and was taking bets. The regatta was an annual affair, a red-letter day on An Cheathrú Rua's mostly black calendar, and it usually drew a large and festive crowd.

We all listened to the weekend forecast with our fingers crossed; it said to expect fine and dry weather. Accepting that leprechauns could knock over ink bottles in classrooms and that fairy people made their homes at the bottoms of gardens was easier than believing most meteorological reports in Ireland, but we lived in hope. I put my money on the big hooker with the reddest sails and held my breath.

On Friday I asked Bridey what time the regatta was scheduled to start the following morning and she looked doubtful. 'I'm not sure it's to be held,' she said. 'I heard a woman at the checkout counter in the Spar say that they'd cancelled it this year because of the accident.' We'd all heard about the tragedy. Apparently two young men not wearing life jackets had drowned the previous year when their boat had tipped over. I asked a secretary at the centre about the upcoming race and the bad news was confirmed: out of respect to the victims' families, the event had indeed been called off.

In the old days in Connemara and other areas of coastal Ireland, someone who fell from a boat and was drowning would not be saved. In fact they *could* not be rescued. People believed that the wee folk were making their claim and anyone trying to rescue a drowning person would meet the same fate, that was for certain. Seán had told me of a tale he'd heard when he was young about fishermen taking a hatchet to the hands of a man as he clung to the side of the *currach*, so powerful was the belief in the ability of these little people to exact revenge on interlopers. One of the students in class had recently learned that her grandfather had drowned along with seven others in Galway Bay, just off the Claddagh, almost a century before as people on shore stood and watched helplessly – at least in their minds.

No-one believed even for a moment that such old superstitions persisted – this was the New Ireland, after all, purged of hocus-pocus and purgatory – but some of us still had water on the brain. We'd also put too much faith in the weather forecast once again; it was drizzling over the hills and looked like coming in our direction on the morning of the aborted regatta. The beach would not be an option – that much was clear – but we wanted a day out. Someone said there was a concession on kayaks for rent farther north along the bay. Four of us trooped through the empty campsite and down to the shore to investigate.

The kayaks were owned by a Breton who had spent most of his recent summers in An Cheathrú Rua. The season so far had been slow and he looked pleased to see us. We tried to practise a little Irish on him, but he just shook his head. 'I've never had time to learn the language,' he said, 'but I will one day.' He looked like he still had more than a few years ahead of him for that, as long as people kept coming to kayak off the Connemara coast.

The other members of our little group had kayaked before; Kate was almost a pro. They quickly shed their shoes and socks, storing them in the Breton's Mini parked on the edge of the water, and took off immediately in a 'V' formation, leaving our leader and me stuck behind. I'd never sat in one of the unstable-looking shells before but with some protracted instruction in a mixture of English and French, I managed to slide myself over the paddle and into the cockpit. In seconds I too was skimming along the surface of the water.

Making my way towards the centre of the bay to join the others felt as simple as walking, with the paddle pulling itself forward to the right and then the left effortlessly. I was making progress without even trying. Perhaps some ancestor in the distant past had made his way from landlocked Roscommon to the sea or had rowed as carefree as the others among the islets of Lough Ree.

I knew I couldn't go straight forever and would have to turn at some point so I leaned to one side as I'd watched the others do and gave the paddle a deep stroke. I'd tilted too far – I could feel that immediately – and frantically tried to regain my balance. No chance, I'd capsized and was standing with the water up to my shoulders, my feet stuck in the dark mud below. 'Think of it as your baptism,' said our man the Breton as he paddled over to help me turn the kayak right side up and retrieve the paddle riding on the current. 'You'll do it just once. One time will be enough and you will learn.' I wasn't so sure that I would, but I was relieved to see he didn't have a hatchet in his hands.

It was a chilly tour of the upper reaches of the Bay of the Great Man in my wet jeans and T-shirt but enjoyable nonetheless as we followed narrow channels clogged with seaweed, explored coves and circled round the little islands. I was afraid of falling in again, not so much because the sea would get a tighter grip on me this time but for egotistical reasons. My three companions, who had thoroughly enjoyed my dunking, were still teasing me, gnashing their teeth together and calling out 'Timber me shivers'. I stayed frozen to the seat, looping rather than turning towards them, and acting like I knew what I was doing. I reached the shore and the parked Mini before they did, not so much because I'd learned the finer points of kayaking but because I was anxious to get my feet back on terra firma.

When I'd cycled back to Doire Fhatharta Mór, hoping along the way that the breeze would dry all the evidence of my spill, Seán and Bridey's eldest son, Shane, greeted me in the driveway. 'I heard you fell in the water,' he said with a smile. 'You'll be having to get out of those wet clothes before you catch your death.' Shane was in his late teens, no longer boy and not quite man, and had returned the night before from a massive rave in Dublin that had been advertised on the radio and in the newspapers for weeks. His words sounded out of character somehow; they didn't sound like something a lad would say. But nothing was ever predictable in An Cheathrú Rua – nothing but the speed at which news seemed to travel.

I should have gone dancing instead. That's what a handful of students did in the evening a couple of times a week. *Damhsa Gaelach* (Irish dancing) was yet another one of the extracurricular activities available at the centre, and its aficionados took it very seriously indeed. I'd sometimes hear them stomping on the wooden floor of the large *halla* and poke my head through the door to see what complex new step they were trying out. Kit, a tall, very thin African-American from Boston whose command of Irish was among the best of all the students, would be shouting '*Luascadh, luascadh!* (Swing, swing!)' with a broad grin above the taped music, and the couples would twirl each other around in complicated patterns, then stop abruptly. They were learning Connemara set dancing and spoke of the even more difficult Kerry version in reverential tones. It all looked hard to me.

The dancers were always seeking out new partners to make up the numbers, especially males, and this became a matter of urgency as the Oíche Mhór Cheoil approached. Dancing just didn't seem to do it for the men as it did for the women, and sometimes two of them would have to dance together as a couple. It reminded me of the Sunday school dances I'd attended in junior high school after I'd left Saint Agatha's for public school but was still required by my parents to receive religious instruction. A few of the more courageous boys would be spinning around on the floor but most of us stood on the sidelines watching the girls have fun.

Under pressure from Kit, I gave it a go one evening and danced with Kate. The others soon saw what I'd known all along: I had not two but a multitude of left feet that wouldn't have been able to locate the right position on the dance floor even if it had been outlined in neon and I'd been handed a detailed map. I'd trip or offer the wrong hand and kept turning to face the window or the chalkboard instead of my partner. It was clear to all that I was not a *damhsóir* now and certainly would not become one in time for the Big Music Night.

I could always try singing again, happy songs like the one about the lovely Peggy from Lettermore, nostalgic melodies about crossing the waves to return to Ireland one day, soft lullabies with nonsense words about giving the old man fresh meat, a hen's egg, a drop of whiskey. Maybe I could manage joining in this time but I doubted it. *Amhránaíocht* (singing) was a popular event on Monday afternoons and attracted some strong talent among the group. I'd joined the first session and was so mesmerised by the harmonies led by Morgan that it was as if I had been struck dumb and could only listen. It was pointless for me to go again into this domain of angels. I'd have to stick to words.

I was too busy in the last couple of weeks of the course to think much about Alice, and she never came to visit, not even when I was alone in my little room and trying to put some order to my dreams or when guarding my turf on the Beach in the Middle. At first I wondered whether she'd left me and Ireland altogether, but the more I thought about it, the less likely that seemed. Alice was off somewhere pouting, I just knew it. We'd had what the language centre's namesake, the writer Máirtín Ó Cadhain, had called *an gnáthghalar Gaelach, scoilteadh* (the chronic Irish disease, a rift). She was counting on me to make it right no matter when or where I chose to do it. The onus was on me. '*Go hIfreann léi* (To hell with her),' I said to myself. She'd be waiting a month of Sundays if that was what she expected.

Alice argued with people. Maybe it was a legacy handed down by the belligerent fairy people. I'd heard that the favoured occupation among them was fighting; a good fight was loved for its own sake. Alice called them 'differences of opinion', not 'fights'. She'd have arguments with her sisters, including my mother, and then she'd give them the silent treatment – the 'no-talkies' – until the other party rectified the situation. 'It gets me blood moving,' she once told me, making as if she were joking, but I knew she believed what she was saying. I didn't remember her ever fighting – or having a difference of opinion, rather – with me in the past. This was something new.

Well, it didn't matter; I'd lost the ability and the will to tangle anyway. I'd lived too long with someone who would close his eyes at the hint of a dispute or head for the nearest door, leaving me to rant at the four walls. I tried that for a while but discovered soon enough how unsatisfying a temper tantrum was without an audience. It was far more successful (and peaceful) to bring up touchy subjects when we were jolly.

Maybe I'd just tell Alice about the kayak adventure the next time she paid a call on me and how I could still feel the mud oozing between my toes. That would smooth the old bird's ruffled feathers. She'd also like the story about how I'd left my bank card in the ATM at the Spar after retrieving the notes and had to wait for the mobile bank truck that visited An Cheathrú Rua a couple of times a week to deliver it back from Galway. 'You awmadawn, you,' she'd say with a laugh. I wanted to hear Alice laugh again and I could make her do it. I just didn't know how to get her to come back.

The last day of class kicked off a series of tributes, farewells and pledges to keep in touch – *as Gaeilge, cinnte* (in Irish, certainly) – that would last until almost dawn the following day. Nuala raced us through grammatical forms we hadn't had time to cover, such as the passive voice, and scattered idioms like seed that might sprout and be of some use someday, somehow. 'The cows have longer horns overseas' was the appropriate Irish substitute for 'The grass is always greener on the other side of the fence'. Just how much greener could grass be than the forty shades you'd find elsewhere in Ireland?

It all came too fast on that last day in the centre but the time had come. '*A Stiofáin*, what will you be doing between now and Christmas?' Nuala asked me. 'What will you be doing in the new year?' *Ach*, the newly introduced future tense. It was only marginally less frightening than the wail of a banshee and jumbled dreams. I couldn't answer just then. Every time I tried to say 'will go', it came out 'went'; I was still in the past. Nuala moved on to someone else who clearly had the future in hand.

I excused myself from class to fetch my roving bank card and when I'd returned the students had turned the tables on the teacher. A game of Fiche Ceist (Twenty Questions) was in progress. Morgan was asking Nuala what she would be doing between then and Christmas and in the new year, about herself and her family – moving easily between the past, the present and the future. The sheep had been rounded up and were all bleating together in Irish. The bellwether looked pleased with the flock but a little abashed at all the personal questions. We were being mischievous kids – she was still the teacher.

The interrogation was brought to a halt with the presentation of a gift – some bauble from a local silversmith – and a song composed by several students with the help of one of the other teachers. It was a clever ditty, 'An Múinteoir Álainn (The Beautiful Teacher)', comparing Nuala with the pirate queen Grace O'Malley and the legendary Deirdre, and extolling how the 'Pearl of Ballyferriter' had taught us the copula and the future tense. Well, some of us, anyway . . .

'Won't you say something on Nuala's behalf?' asked Marsha. I looked at her in surprise. 'You're never at a loss for words,' she said with a grin. That was true in English. Gab had been a gift – or a scourge, depending on your viewpoint – bestowed on me from the start. I wasn't so sure it applied in Irish though. I looked to the class clown, the over-achiever, the academic; they all had something wittier, more ambitious or smarter to say than me in the past, present *and* the future. But there was no escape this time; all eyes were on me.

Coincidentally I thought I might have something that would

keep me firmly afloat in this particular kayak. I'd spent the previous afternoon on the Beach in the Middle on my own, stringing sentences together and was pleased with the way things were working out. I'd figured that if I wasn't a singer, most certainly was not a dancer, and couldn't even beat in time with a pair of spoons, I could at least try to put a few words together as my set piece for the Big Music Night.

It wasn't going to be a poem – metre and rhyme schemes in Irish would elude me for decades, I was certain – but a kind of speech on why I'd come to Connemara to learn the language might go down well. Why not? It was a topic on everyone's mind and had been mulled over ad infinitum since the start of the course. Now in class I could just substitute 'I' for 'we' and see how it all panned out. This could be a test run before I had it all made perfect and packaged it up for the main event with some help from Bridey. Who just happened to have my notes with her at that moment. I'd just have to wing it, I thought, and faltered my way through a protracted 'thank you'.

We all dispersed after the last class. A few went to do some last-minute cramming before the final exams later in the afternoon, many home to pack, and others headed for An Chistin's picnic tables. I went back to the Beach in the Middle for one last look at the cormorants, the horseshoe crabs and the Aran Islands, and to correct a few mistakes. From my rocky chair I watched a woman in the distance walking towards me. She paused and looked down, flipping something over with her foot. I felt my stomach flip-flop. But as she approached I could see she was wearing a Manchester United T-shirt. Hardly my Aunt Alice's style. I'd leave the Beach in the Middle for the last time without seeing her.

The Big Music Night was as Irish an event as could be: slightly disorganised, something for everyone, all ages represented. Steam trays and platters offered up the kind of stodge we'd all become familiar with in varying shades of white, grey and pink, but most people made straight for the bar, ordering pints and half 'uns of Paddy's for friends, colleagues, lodgers and hosts.

We sat at long, crowded tables, empty pint glasses sprouting up all around us like weeds as we joked and played games. They were foolish pastimes, the sort you engage in at age ten or thereabouts, but classes were over, exams had ended and this was our last chance to be kids again. I could fold napkins in the shape of a crown; everyone had their own lyrics – silly or smutty – for 'When Irish Eyes are Smiling'. Chris wanted to know what animal each person would be if the goddess of anthropomorphism descended and waved her magic wand over the tables. Herons, gazelles and angelfish at our table – lizards, turtles and warthogs for people at tables out of earshot. I ended up an emperor penguin, a creature I'd never heard of. Kate told me that it was a large, dignified penguin that, unlike other species, made its home in only one place: Antarctica. I liked the sound of that.

All the while students were performing their set pieces up on stage. The Big Music Night reminded me of a Chinese opera, with members of the audience eating, drinking and socialising, paying attention only to the acts that interested them or that they'd decided had talent. The Super Celt sang 'Danny Boy' in a rich baritone with a soprano from the beginners' class. The dancers, led by Kit dressed in a kilt, stomped and twirled like tops; they were awarded with a prolonged round of applause. Beth performed one of her own songs in English while beating a tambourine and then switched to a sombre *sean-nós* song in Irish. At the table next to ours the staff from the centre listened intently, their faces blank. It was impossible to tell whether they were enraptured or listening for mistakes.

Seán and Bridey arrived late – they'd had furniture to deliver somewhere up in north Connemara – and came over to the table to greet us. Bridey was wearing a blouse with zebra stripes, and I wanted to tell her we'd already chosen a nice animal for her but I couldn't remember which one it had been. They shouted a round of drinks for all of us, including me provided I agreed not to ride my bicycle back, lest the stone walls close in on me and I found myself at the back of a field living among the *daoine sí*. I was surprised to see their son Shane behind the bar pulling the pints and he gave me a wink.

'Tell me how your piece went,' said Bridey enthusiastically as she handed me a drink. 'Did you also say it in English like you said you might?' It was only then that I realised I'd never been called to the stage. We'd been so wrapped up with silly games, the singers, the dancers and a harpist who had silenced the room with her playing that I'd forgotten all about the speech. Had I given my name to the master of ceremonies that evening? Was I supposed to? Bridey started to say she might have a word with him, but I could see that the MC, a dapper older man who always sounded like he was speaking Irish even when he spoke English, was well into his cups. One of the Southern boys from the beginners' class was singing the praises of Lord Jesus and softly strumming on a guitar as last call was sounded. Soon we'd hear the 'Soldier's Song' and the crowd would began to disperse. It was too late. I'd missed my chance but I didn't think it really mattered anymore. What I'd learned would stay with me; there would be other opportunities.

We stood outside the hotel, rocking on our heels and trying to decide our next move. The first bus would leave the centre for Galway early the next morning and the second one a couple of hours after that. We had stretched our drinking-up time to well beyond last call; it was late but no-one wanted to enter into another round of goodbyes and pledges just then. There would be plenty of time for that later.

Without calling out their destination, a small group began to head in the direction of the sea. I left my bicycle firmly chained to a post in the hotel parking lot and followed them down the dark road that led to Coral Beach. We'd said almost everything we had to say by then and were plodding along in silence when Beth began to sing a song called 'An Mhaighdean Mhara'. It was about a merrow, or a silkie, who had married a mortal when he'd taken away her magic cloak, but must return to the sea now that it had been found.

'It seems that you have faded away and abandoned the love of life/The snow is spread about at the mouth of the sea,' Beth sang. 'The night is dark and the wind is high/The plough can be seen high in the sky/But on top of the waves and by the mouth of the sea/we give you Mary Chinidh to swim forever . . .' Though she sang it sweetly and expertly, 'The Mermaid' was a very doleful song and I begged her to stop. I'd recently tried to wade through a poem by Nuala Ní Dhomhnaill, which likened the loss of Irish to a mermaid on dry land; when the mermaid stands up and tries to walk, she stumbles and falls down. I was feeling out of water now too.

We could hear voices as we reached the top of the hill and they grew louder as we descended to the sea. My mind raced to the Famine graveyard and Alice's admonition to avoid it by sticking to the shoreline and listening to the surf. But it was very dark – the sky *chomh dubh le tóin phúca*, or 'as black as a devil's arse' – and I couldn't see my feet much less the entrance to Children's Beach. I'd stick to the road with the others for the time being; they appeared to know their way.

As we came closer to Coral Beach we could see the source of the voices. A group of backpackers was sitting on a narrow rock just above the water. They waved and one of them called out for us to join them. The sea breeze carried the acrid scent of hashish and unwashed clothes with just a hint of cologne. Four of us followed it to the top of the rock.

They were five Bretons on holiday; the Bord Fáilte, the national tourist office, must have been working overtime in western France that summer. 'Are you looking for your ancestors?' I asked them, expecting a laugh, but they said nothing. They were much too busy opening tins of Harp and mixing razor-thin slivers of hashish with a black tobacco that smelled like cow dung. A woman with long blond hair offered us some of both with a welcoming gesture.

Beth had decided she'd speak only Irish on her last night in the Gaeltacht. She was catching the earlier bus and heading straight back to America for a wedding; she hadn't a moment to lose and asked Kate whether she would be on the same bus.

'What language are they speaking?' asked one of the back-packers. He was a dark-haired young man with a goatee and a twirled moustache that must have prevented him from getting too close to almost everything. He seemed to be the only one who knew English. 'Is it Arabic?'

So much for distant relations, I thought. But Alice had said she thought it sounded like Jewish to her. Hadn't one eighteenth-century antiquarian tried to establish a link between Irish and Maltese? Maybe there was something to it after all.

I told the Dalí lookalike that Beth was speaking Irish and that we'd been studying the language here in the Gaeltacht. He didn't ask me why but said he'd like to hear some more. I was about to suggest to Beth that she sing him one of the less mournful verses of the mermaid song, but then I realised that my big chance was at hand. Like a flash I had my scribbled notes in hand.

'*An dhaoine uaisle* (Ladies and gentlemen),' I began, '*ba mhaith liom óráid an-ghearr a tabhairt as Gaeilge* (I'd like to give a very short speech in Irish).' The other Bretons began to mumble in French but continued to worry their cans of lager and spliffs.

'*An-mhaith, ar aghaidh leat!*' Beth cried, urging me on, and both Chris and Kate gave me a thumbs-up.

'*Ní ceolteoir mé agus ní damhsóir mé. Is ach iriseoir mé marsin scríobh mé cúpla abairt dom féin. Tá sé tábhachtacht dom* (I'm not a singer or a dancer. I'm just a writer so I've written a few sentences about myself. This is important to me).' I stood with my back towards the shore, barely able to keep my balance in the wind after a long evening of festivities. I didn't dare look down but gazed over to the darkened shoreline of Garomna.

'*A fhir agus a mhná na hÉireann! In ainm Dé agus in ainm na nglún a chuaigh romhainn . . .*' Now it was our group's turn to start mumbling and I heard a couple of exaggerated groans. Okay, echo-ing the Proclamation of the Irish Republic, the call to arms pub-lished on the morning of the Easter Rising, may have been a bit melodramatic and hardly applied to this lot of foreigners anyway.

But I liked the sound of it, the stirring tone, and my moment had arrived: 'Irishmen and Irishwomen! In the name of Ó God and the dead generations . . .'

'What are you saying?' asked Dalí. 'It is very strange for us.' I didn't bother answering him. What difference did it make whether he understood the words? This was for me and I was on my way. '*Tá an eachtrannach ag labhairt Gaeilge* (The foreigner is speaking Irish).'

One of the Bretons began scrunching up his empty beer can. It made a hollow, familiar sound. I hoped he wasn't going to throw it at me.

'*Nuair a tháinig mé anseo go Conamara, ní raibh focal Gaeilge agam. Ceart go leor, níl sé sin fíor ar fad* . . . (When I came here to Connemara, I didn't speak any Irish. Okay, that's not entirely true . . .)' I looked down to the others fidgeting uncomfortably. Beth smiled and nodded her head so I carried on.

'*Nuair a bhí mé an-óg – fadó, fadó, fadó! – mhúin m'aintín, Alice, dom mé féin a choisreacan as Gaeilge agus is cuimhin liom é fós* . . . (When I was very young – a long, long, long time ago! – my Aunt Alice taught me how to bless myself and I remember it still . . .)' Beth and the others in the group began to giggle as I repeated how I'd learned to pronounce the sign of the cross while sitting on Alice's lap: 'Enormana knocker, August a vick, August a spread knave, Almond.' It did sound funny now, but it was history and I'd always remember it that way.

Four of the Bretons began scrambling down the rock and hit the sand with a thud. 'He isn't the teacher, is he?' asked the blonde of her companion. Maybe *fadó* meant something similar in Breton.

'*Ach ní raibh ann ach fuaim – glór gan ciall – rud marbh cosúil leis na nglún a chuaigh romhainn. Is teanga bheo anois í dom an Ghaeilge* . . . (But it was just sound – sound without meaning – as dead as all those generations that came before us. Irish is alive for me now . . .)'

Chris let out a whoop.

'*Agus labhróidh mé í – labhróimid uile í – ar son na mairbh agus na beo agus dóibh siúd nár rugadh go fóill. Ó a Dhia, ó a*

Dhia, tá an eachtrannach ag labhairt Gaeilge faoi dheireadh (And I will speak it – we will all speak it – for the dead and the living and the unborn. Oh, God, oh God, the foreigner is speaking Irish at last).'

Dalí stood up and faced me. 'Monsieur,' he said, 'I didn't understand a fucking word you said. *Bonne chance.*' With that he was gone. They were all gone now but I didn't care. I'd said what I had to. I was finished.

My companions and I sat on the rock in silence, sipping on the last of the Harps that the Bretons had left behind in their haste to flee the 'sound without meaning'. The wind had died down and the sea was calm, but by the time our supplies had run out we were cold and tired. 'Who feels like heading back?' someone asked, and the rest of us moaned. The walk back to the centre and our various houses was too long, too exhausting to contemplate at the moment. Perhaps we could wait until one of the pairs of lovers in the parked cars at the far end of the beach had reached their conclusions, started their engines and began to make their way up the hill again. We could beg a lift; there would probably be room for a small group of foreigners at this late hour.

We lay down on the rock, all four of us, entwined like a lump of deep-fried whitebait that couldn't let go. When I closed my eyes, I felt unsteady and my head began to spin. I opened them and looked down at the swell, feeling even dizzier. The others must have been experiencing the same thing because they all started to giggle.

'This is like being on a roller coaster,' said Beth, and everyone started to laugh uncontrollably. 'What a balancing act!' The great pretzel of arms and legs began to sway. 'Steady, steady,' I shouted and tried to hold onto the rock but grabbed Kate's foot instead. It was too late. I fell into the water first, taking Kate with me, and the other two followed. As we hit the surface, our weight disturbed the phosphorescence, making great starbursts in the black sea.

We stood in the waist-high water, shocked by the unexpected plunge. 'Now that's what I call a baptism!' said Chris, but the rest of us were too mesmerised by the electric dance surrounding us to respond. It was only when I began to shiver that I stumbled around the rock to get back to the beach and throw myself onto the sand.

As I got closer to the shore I glanced up and saw Alice at the top of the hill looking down at me. I began running towards her but stumbled and when I looked up again she wasn't there. I walked over to the same rock where I'd spotted her that afternoon on the first day of class, sat down and put my head in my hands. I did want to see Alice again. I'd been thinking about her a lot over the past couple of days and I was anxious to make amends. What was the point of this squabbling? She was my Aunt Alice and I liked everything about her. I always had and I always would.

I heard a discreet cough and turned around. Alice was standing almost directly behind me. She was dressed in her travelling outfit, as she had been when we first met up in Dublin, and had her hand on her hip, her fingers splayed. The pose reminded me of the mock-defensive one Lucille Ball would strike, her eyes flashing, in 'I Love Lucy' when Ricky Ricardo was about to chide her for doing something silly again. It was a funny stance, one that always made me laugh, but I contained myself. I didn't want Alice to get the wrong idea.

'Hello, stranger,' I said, just a teensy bit distant. 'Long time, no see.' She didn't acknowledge the greeting but just looked me over and said: 'Thank you for that.'

'For what?' I asked her. 'Oh, falling into the sea? I knew you'd find *that* funny but we didn't do it on purpose. And can you believe it's the second time in a week? I was in a kayak with some of the others on Saturday and . . .'

Alice interrupted me mid-sentence. 'I know that, Ste. I've been around, waiting for you. I asked Shane, dear boy, to tell you to get out of those wet clothes before you caught cold. You never know what's good for you. Lucky for you I'm here to remind you every once in a while.' She smiled broadly to show me she was joking, and I stuck my tongue out at her. 'No, Mr Too-Big-for-His-Breeches. I was thanking you for what you said about me in your speech.'

With the fall and seeing Alice again, the speech and the reference to my aunt hadn't crossed my mind. 'I didn't make it just to get you to come back, Al. I said it because it's true.'

Alice remained silent but I knew what she was thinking. It was the same thing in the end. She knew what was good for me and maybe I knew a thing or two about what was good for her. 'What will you do now?' she asked.

'I might go and study Icelandic,' I teased her. 'I hear Reykjavik is pretty fine this time of year. Long nights, great club scene, Björk. I'm sure we've got ancestors up there too, what with all the blondes in the family.'

Her eyes darkened. 'What are you blithering on about, wise guy? You're going home now, and you know where that is.'

Of course I knew where home was – I was searching my pockets for the mobile phone – but I wondered about her. Where was she going? 'The like of me will never be *here* again,' she said, as if reading my mind. 'But it's been a pretty good ride, *nach bhfuil*?'

I was startled by what I'd heard. 'So you have learned some of the Gaelic along the way,' I turned to say. 'Oh, you're a sly divil, Al.' But she wasn't there. She'd vanished just like that. Once again.

The phone was in my top pocket stuffed beneath a sodden ball of notepaper. It was wet and sticky from the phosphorus and the sea water and wouldn't switch on. 'Maybe these things dry out,' I thought to myself, and put it back in my pocket. I sat for a while, wondering whether Alice would come back, but she stayed away so I got up and walked down to the sea.

The others weren't on the beach so I climbed up the rock to have a look there. They must have found a pair of lovers to take them all home; there was no-one there either. I leaned over to look down at the surf and the mobile phone slipped out of my shirt pocket and into the sea, lighting up like a flame as it fell through the phosphorous to the bottom. 'Good riddance,' I thought to myself. I wouldn't be needing it anymore, even if it still worked. I was going home.

I haven't seen a lot of Alice since that late summer night on the south Connemara coast. She visits from time to time but only stays for a moment and never says much. She'd travel with me again if I needed her – or she needed me. There's no doubt about that. But I'd have to issue an unequivocal invitation this time. Oh, and we'd have to meet halfway. She never did like London much.

Bibliography

Akenson, Donald Harman. *The Irish Diaspora: A Primer*. P.D. Meany Toronto and The Institute of Irish Studies, The Queen's University of Belfast, Toronto and Belfast, 1996.

Ardagh, John. *Ireland and the Irish: Portrait of a Changing Society*. Penguin, London, 1995.

Coogan, Tim Pat. *Wherever Green Is Worn: The Story of the Irish Diaspora*. Hutchinson, London, 2000.

Crowley, Tony. *The Politics of Language in Ireland: 1366–1922*. Routledge, London, 2000.

Curley, Helen (ed.). *Local Ireland Almanac and Yearbook of Facts 2000*. Local Ireland, Dublin, 1999.

Delaney, Frank. *The Celts*. Grafton Books, London, 1989.

Hindley, Reg. *The Death of the Irish Language: A Qualified Obituary*. Routledge, London, 1990.

Kennedy, Conan. *Irish Language Ireland*. Morrigan Books, Killala, County Mayo, 1998.

O'Brien, Flann. *The Poor Mouth*. Flamingo, London, 1993.

Ó Ciosáin, Éamon. *Buried Alive: A Reply to The Death of the Irish Language*. Dáil Uí Chadhain, Dublin, 1991.

O'Crohan, Tomás. *The Islandman*. Oxford University Press, Oxford, 2000.

O'Faolain, Sean. *The Irish*. Penguin, London, 1984.

Ó Murchú, Helen. *Irish: Facing the Future*. European Bureau for Lesser Used Languages, Dublin, 1999.

O'Sullivan, Maurice. *Twenty Years A-Growing*. Oxford University Press, Oxford, 2000.

Pearse, Pádraic. *Short Stories*. Mercier Press, Cork, 1985.

Purdon, Edward. *The Story of the Irish Language*. Mercier Press, Cork, 1999.

Robinson, Tim. *Connemara: Introduction and Gazetteer*. Folding Landscapes, Roundstone, County Galway, 1990.

Robinson, Tim. *Oileáin Árann*. Folding Landscapes, Roundstone, County Galway, 1996.

Synge, J.M. *The Aran Islands*. Oxford University Press, Oxford, 1987.

Willimas, J.E. Caerwyn and Patrick K. Ford. *The Irish Literary Tradition*. University of Wales, Cardiff, 1997.

LONELY PLANET JOURNEYS

JOURNEYS is a unique collection of travel writing – published by the company that understands travel better than anyone else.

It is a series for anyone who has ever experienced – or dreamed of – the magical moment when they encountered a strange culture or saw a place for the first time. They are tales to read while you're planning a trip, while you're on the road or while you're in an armchair, in front of a fire.

These outstanding titles explore our planet through the eyes of a diverse group of international writers. JOURNEYS books catch the spirit of a place, illuminate a culture, recount an adventure, or introduce a fascinating way of life. They always entertain, and always enrich the experience of travel.

'Lively, intelligent and varied . . . an important contribution to travel literature' – *Age (Melbourne)*

SUPERCARGO
A Journey Among Ports
Thornton McCamish

Thornton McCamish sets out from London in search of whatever remains of the rough-and-ready life of those who work and travel by water. As he circles the Mediterranean and follows ancient spice and slaver routes around Cape Horn and across the Indian Ocean, he finds, instead of sea dogs and old salts, bad food, themed bars, model ships and prostitutes.